# Masters at Work

MASTERS AT WORK

# BECOMING A SOMMELIER

ROSIE SCHAAP

SIMON & SCHUSTER

*New York   London   Toronto   Sydney   New Delhi*

Simon & Schuster
1230 Avenue of the Americas
New York, NY 10020

First Simon & Schuster hardcover edition September 2019

SIMON & SCHUSTER and colophon are registered trademarks of
Simon & Schuster, Inc.

For information about special discounts for bulk purchases,
please contact Simon & Schuster Special Sales at 1-866-506-1949
or business@simonandschuster.com.

The Simon & Schuster Speakers Bureau can bring authors to your
live event. For more information or to book an event, contact the
Simon & Schuster Speakers Bureau at 1-866-248-3049
or visit our website at www.simonspeakers.com.

Manufactured in the United States of America

1   3   5   7   9   10   8   6   4   2

Library of Congress Cataloging-in-Publication Data is available.

ISBN 978-1-9821-2041-2
ISBN 978-1-9821-2042-9 (ebook)

FOR DAEL,

WHO LOVES WINE,

WHO IS A STEADFAST FRIEND

# CONTENTS

# INTRODUCTION

There's a story in my family that dates my connection to wine to an early age. I must have been three or four years old. My parents took a quick vacation and left me in the care of their friend Pat, a glamorous and indulgent honorary aunt whom I adored. Imagine a sort of Mary Poppins type—if Mary Poppins had been a patrician Back Bay Bostonian with expensive taste in wine, who drank a lot of it.

When my mother and father returned from their trip, Pat greeted them at the door to our apartment with me in her arms. In the telling of the story that they passed down to me when I was old enough to appreciate it, I looked up at my parents and earnestly asked, "Bordeaux?"

Since then, I have sometimes wondered: How formative was that long weekend with Pat? Was it a defining moment? Did it set the rest of my life on an irreversible course? Who knows?

Until now, I've written more about spirits and cocktails than I have about wine, but the truth is that where drinking is concerned, I have always been a wine drinker and wine lover above all else. Of course I love a beautifully made, ice-cold martini—and I suspect that there are some people in my life who might never want to talk to me again for saying this—but I'd be okay if I never drank one again.

That's not how I feel about wine, which I regard as a more essential, everyday pleasure. At the end of a long day, like many people I know, I pour myself some wine—not a shot of tequila. It's not often that I crave a cocktail with my dinner, but I almost always want a glass or two of wine with it.

However, none of this makes me an authority on wine. The absolute barest essentials of how wine comes into being (grapes are picked, they are crushed, they are fermented, the alcoholic juice produced by fermentation is aged and bottled) may have not changed dramatically over its long history, but it is nonetheless a vast and ancient subject, one that takes years, maybe a lifetime, to master, if mastery is even possible. More than sixty countries produce wine for consumer markets. California alone makes more than seventeen million gallons of the stuff every year. According to the most recent statistics on the website of the Wine Institute, an advocacy and public policy organization representing one thousand California wineries, Americans consumed 949 million gallons of wine in 2016—a significant increase from the previous year's 922 million, and nearly double the amount consumed twenty years earlier.

And the subject assumes an even more daunting cast when I consider that virtually every country, every region, every micro-region that brings wine into being has its own ways of producing, naming, and describing it. When an American customer steps into a wine shop or reads a restaurant's wine list, he or she often encounters a geographically organized system focused on the best-known wine-producing countries, which include Australia, France, Germany, Italy, and Spain, broken down further into sub-regions. But now, in more comprehensive shops and restaurants, he or she might also be asked to consider wines from the Czech Republic, Greece, Hungary, Lebanon, Portugal, and Switzerland, among other nations, all of which have long and distinguished histories of winemaking, even if their output hasn't been well known here.

Still, it is usually the case that, when I'm out having

dinner with friends at a nice restaurant, everyone looks at me hopefully when the wine list arrives at the table, as though I'm an expert. "Why don't *you* take a look?" they ask. This is because they know that much of my professional life has been devoted to writing about the pleasures of drinking. What my friends fail to acknowledge is that this doesn't make me a wine expert, either. Sharing a recipe for a perfect Manhattan is one thing; parsing the innumerable distinctions among the many villages, vineyards, and vintages of Burgundy is another thing entirely.

The wine list—often a hulking, leather-bound volume spanning dozens of pages—is an object I've seen strike terror, or at least stir up anxiety, in the hearts of otherwise confident and sophisticated adults, including well-known food writers and restaurant critics. Fortunately, somewhere in the room there is a real, genuine, authentic expert to help us read and interpret it: the sommelier (in places that prefer to dispense with old-fashioned French formalities, this person is instead sometimes called the wine steward). The problem is that most people I know are even more afraid of the sommelier than they are of the list; he or she often inspires a certain look that crosses their faces, a look they might not have worn since middle school math class, a look that says: *Don't call on me. Don't call on me. Don't call on me.*

I really wish people didn't feel that way. No one should be afraid of a sommelier. Wine is a pleasure, and in its pursuit there should be no snobbery, no condescension, no pain, no fear. The sommelier is there to help us, to teach us, to guide us. I always know that I stand to learn a lot from a conversation with a good sommelier, and that the best sommeliers I've encountered have a gift for assuaging anxiety instantly, by making their impromptu tableside lessons lively and engaging exchanges.

So what is a sommelier, anyway? For better or worse, the job eludes precise description, as what exactly a sommelier does can vary considerably from restaurant to restaurant. *The Oxford Companion to Wine* tells us that the "sommelier's job is to ensure that any wine ordered is served correctly and, ideally, to advise on the individual characteristics of every wine on the establishment's wine list and on food and wine matching. In some establishments, the sommelier may also be responsible for compiling the list, buying and storing the wine, and restocking whatever passes for a cellar." Even this expansive, reliable doorstopper of a reference book evades the profession's complicated history.

In her book *Cork Dork: A Wine-Fueled Adventure Among the Obsessive Sommeliers, Big Bottle Hunters, and Rogue Scientists Who Taught Me to Live for Taste*, Bianca Bosker subjects it to a far more thorough treatment, tracing sommeliers all the way back to Pharaoh's cupbearer in the biblical book of Genesis. But the development of the sommelier's vocation as we now know it started to take shape much later. "The job of 'sommelier' became official in 1318 under a decree by France's King Philip the Tall, though for a few hundred years, it required managing the pack animals, *bêtes de somme*, that transported things between households," Bosker writes. "By the seventeenth century, somms had been promoted: A *grand seigneur* would have a *bouteiller* to stock and store his wines, a sommelier to select and set them out for the table, and an *échanson* to serve them." In the centuries since then, it appears that those *bouteiller*s and *échanson*s were made redundant, so to speak, and that sommeliers absorbed the tasks that had once been theirs. Sommeliers are now generally understood to be responsible for stocking, storing, selecting, and serving wines—but in restaurants (which they predate), not in the households of *grand seigneurs*, rich men.

When I spoke with Eric Asimov, the chief wine critic for the *New York Times*, we agreed that even as anxiety about talking with sommeliers remains potent, the state of the profession is quite healthy. Until fairly recently, sommeliers were pretty thin on the ground; Asimov's *Times* colleague, Florence Fabricant, pronounced them "an endangered species" in 1986. Now, especially in big cities like New York and Los Angeles, there's an abundance of skillful and knowledgeable sommeliers. "I so much appreciate sommeliers," he told me. "I don't care how much you know about wine: You never know as much about the wine list in a restaurant as a sommelier does. I believe in most circumstances you have to trust the sommelier in a restaurant, and I do."

I do, too. I not only trust them, I'm also grateful to them. They've put in a lot of hours to ensure that they can help me find a wine I'll love that I can afford. And, almost to a person, they have never failed to answer even my weirdest, dumbest questions.

If you've picked up this book, it's not only because you love wine, it's also because you've thought about becoming a sommelier. I have, too. Maybe it's a hazy, soft-focus daydream right now (as it is for me), or maybe you're deep into your study of the subject. The work of the sommelier brings together history, topography, geology, culture, taste, and pleasure: if all of these excite you, and you honestly like working with other people, it could be the perfect job for you. A sommelier who privileges wine over people simply should not be a sommelier.

Maybe you were drawn in this direction by the *Somm* documentaries, or the television series *Uncorked*, or by the book *Cork Dork*—all of which underscore how critical studying is to the sommelier's job, how much there is to learn and to know. But superior skills at memorization, blind tasting, and acing tests, impressive as they are, do not in themselves make great sommeliers. Other qualities— including patience, style, warmth, even empathy—matter, too.

Wherever this book finds you on your way to wine stewardship, I hope you will take inspiration, along with some very practical advice, from the stories of the two remarkable sommeliers profiled in these pages: Roger Dagorn and Amanda Smeltz. The former, now seventy, grew up in a restaurant-owning French family steeped in knowledge about food and wine, and has amassed virtually every honor and qualification available in his profession. The latter is in her early thirties and was raised in central Pennsylvania by parents who never drank wine at all, and in less than a decade in New York she established herself as a star in her field, developing and tending to the cellars and wine lists of some of the city's trendiest and most distinctive restaurants. Their backgrounds, points of view, and professional paths could hardly be more different: One was born in America, the other in France. One wears a suit to work, the other jeans and T-shirts. One went through the grueling certification exams, the other did not. But both are brilliant at what they do, because they hold at least one crucial quality in common: they demonstrate, by example, that the best sommeliers are above all else patient, wise, and generous teachers.

I t's half past four on a late September day, and "family meal" is winding down at Estela, a trendy restaurant in downtown Manhattan. Early autumn's muted, late-afternoon sunlight laps in through the tall windows at the front of the room, giving the marble bar something like a halo, the scuffed-just-so rustic wooden floorboards a warm glow. The family in this case is the restaurant's staff, or many of its thirty-odd members, anyway: cooks, servers, sommeliers— and Estela's wine director, Amanda Smeltz, whom I will trail during tonight's dinner service. For now, I sit on a bar stool and eavesdrop on this convivial scene.

When Barack and Michelle Obama were seen dining

at the intimate, forty-five-seat spot in 2014, the food-focused website *Eater* proclaimed the former the "hippest POTUS of all time" in its headline about the dinner, and the subheadline made clear exactly what sort of place this is: "Forget white tablecloths. Barack and Michelle want some orange wine and mussels escabeche." Its food is known to be delicious in a complex, cerebral way, more about unexpected flavor combinations and surprising textures than obvious pleasures, while still being undeniably pleasurable. And wine—distinctive, arguably unusual wine—is a significant part of the restaurant's identity.

The menu changes often, but tonight it includes those mussels the Obamas might have ordered a few years back, an alluring assemblage of steak with eggplant and black sesame, and one of the restaurant's signature dishes: fried *arroz negro*—black rice—with squid and Romesco. I'd tried this rice and it's insane—one of the most headily flavorful things I've ever eaten. I'm trying hard to resist the overused word *umami*—described by some as the sixth taste sense category, the one that covers otherwise hard-to-classify, intensely savory flavors like anchovies and blue cheese and truffles—but I've never tasted anything to which it more aptly applies than this crazy rice dish. It is rich and strange and addictive: I just kept wanting one more bite, and another, and another. And it seems like a formidable challenge (for me, anyway) to conceive of a wine that might have the backbone to stand up for itself in the presence of so much so-muchness.

There's a lot of laughter around the table during family meal, over big bowls of pasta. But it can't go on much longer: the paying customers will start to arrive in exactly one hour, when the doors open at five thirty. The chefs and the rest of the kitchen crew rise from the table first and return to their stations. The floor and bar staff, including Amanda, lingers just a little longer before springing up. But they're working while their dinner winds down: Amanda starts to fill them in on amendments to tonight's wine list, and brings them up to speed on changes to wines served by the glass (sometimes abbreviated to "BTG"), on what's running low, on what will soon run out entirely (or, in restaurant-speak, what will soon be 86'd), on what's new, and on what she's especially excited about. "Lots of German tonight," she tells them.

"Wunderbar!" a server replies, clapping his hands together.

There is, for example, a Riesling from Hofgut Falkenstein, where Erich Weber and his son Johannes make wines according to rigorously traditional methods. The bottle has a striking label, featuring what looks like a fine woodcut of a large, ancient barn. The liquid Amanda pours from the green bottle is ethereally pale. "Falkenstein," Amanda explains, translates to "Falcon's Rock."

From the depths of my memory, the weirdly triumphalist theme song from the 1980s prime-time soap opera *Falcon Crest*—about a dysfunctional winemaking family in California—leaps forward. I am silently mortified, and I challenge my will to stifle it as quickly as it can. I resolve to focus on every word Amanda says. Fortunately, that's not hard to do: listening to her is fun. I detect more than mere obligation while her colleagues listen to her describing the wines on the list. They're enjoying it, too.

Falkenstein's vineyards, she tells us, nestle in a sloping, treeless valley in the coldest part of the Mosel. There the Webers make "wines of wind and rock," Amanda continues, "wines about brightness and lift."

If you're thinking that most people don't talk like this, you're right, and this is probably where I should tell you that Amanda is a poet. I don't mean that figuratively. She is literally a poet. A bona fide, published poet. And I should also probably tell you that this is one of the main reasons, in a world full of talented and respected sommeliers, I wanted to focus on her.

The selfish part of this is that I love poetry as much as I love wine, and there's no question that I know more about it than I know about wine. The less selfish part is that, because I knew Amanda is both a poet and a sommelier, I sensed that in her I would find someone for whom wine is not everything, or the only thing that matters, and that she would have none of that disturbing automaton quality that had turned me off of some sommeliers I'd seen on television and read about in books and magazines, even some who had served me very good wine. It just seems to me that a life fully lived requires more than wine alone, as wonderful as wine is.

It was, in fact, poetry that brought her to New York City—not wine. When she moved to the city in 2009, it wasn't because she was looking for a big break in high-end hospitality; it was to do a master's of fine arts course in creative writing at the New School University. Her first book of poems, *Imperial Bender*, was published in 2013, and was commended by the *Chicago Tribune* and the Poetry Foundation as one of the year's notable titles in the genre.

Words not only matter more to Amanda than they matter to most sommeliers, they matter more to her than they do to most humans. Her language is both evocative and precise, and her deep, husky voice and distinctive speech pattern bring to my mind the singer and bassist Kim Deal of the Pixies and the Breeders. And with her long and layered dark hair pulled back, and some of her tattoos showing, Amanda looks like she could be an indie rock star, too.

Her Falkenstein lesson sits somewhere between recitation and reverie—but what she doesn't want it to be is a monologue. The floor is open for discussion. Amanda asks one of the servers to talk about the wine's aroma. He inhales and focuses. "Orchard fruits. Gray slate. Soil. It's intensely mineral."

Amanda nods in encouragement. "It tastes like stone," she says. "It's as acidic as a wine can be."

"It's *sooooo* German," her colleague adds.

"There's a sense of coldness," she says, whereas, with other wines, "sometimes one can smell warmth and sun."

Only twelve cases of this wine of wind and rock came to the United States—and four of those were destined for Estela. Amanda is on fire for this wine. I'm reminded of a delightful column by Jay McInerney, called "How to Impress Your Sommelier, Part One," in which he explains:

> *If you're having trouble getting over your fear of sommeliers, here are a few tips on how to make him think you are cool:*
>
> *If sommeliers have a consistent point of snobbery, it's a slight disdain or at least weariness with Chardonnay.*

*Tease yours by asking about Austrian Rieslings. All sommeliers love Austrian Rieslings. Then, bring it on home. Ask him to recommend a German Riesling.*

*Don't roll your eyes. Get over your Blue Nun/Black Tower prejudice.*

Yes, Riesling is among Amanda's favorite grapes. But she avoids using the word on the menu, so that she and the sommeliers and servers under her supervision can avoid what she calls "the sweet/dry conversation." Riesling can be controversial: it's an often misunderstood variety, unable to shake that association, to which McInerney alludes, with the cloying sweetness for which certain well-known, mass-produced Rieslings are loved by some and loathed by others, and to which this Falkenstein bears absolutely no resemblance.

For a wine this good, and this scarce, it's also surprisingly reasonable at $15 a glass. (Currently, the most expensive wine on offer at Estela by the glass is $20, and the least expensive is $11.) And since the relationship between wine and food must always be foremost in a sommelier's mind—with the food leading the way, not the wine—Amanda suggests to the team that it would be great with the tilefish, the corn, the burrata, the crudités, and anything vegetal and herbal. There can be real magic in a just-right pairing, or at least a deeply satisfying sensory synergy, and the sommelier is the person best equipped to make that happen.

Next, she describes a French red, also new to the list: It is made from 100 percent Gamay grapes, grown in a soil of mixed clay and limestone. It has undergone "full carbonic maceration"—a process in which fermentation begins inside unpressed whole clusters of grapes. Guests don't necessarily need to know this in order to enjoy the wine, but Amanda believes that the staff should know as much about each wine as possible. She is unabashedly scholarly in her approach. Knowledge is vital to her, and details matter.

"It's evolved, but light in body," she continues. She'd like to disrupt people's expectations of Gamay—often associated with the florid Beaujolais Nouveau that shows up on many Thanksgiving dinner tables—and show that in its earthier manifestations, it is a serious grape.

The staff has been briefed. The tables set. The lighting lowered. The cellar is in order, and the bottles of wines sold by the glass are in place behind the bar. What remains is to wait for the most important, and unpredictable, element to arrive: the dining public.

———

AMANDA IS THIRTY-THREE, WHICH may sound young to be in a position of major responsibility at a restaurant that has been voted one of the world's fifty best—especially at a restaurant that places an even greater, more defining emphasis on its wine list than do most. The whole staff "has to be on board with wine," she says. "It's almost a prerequisite. That's not true everywhere." And her duties don't end at Estela: Amanda is also the wine director at Café Altro Paradiso, a substantially larger place that is one of Estela's siblings in the same restaurant group.

But she has, if not quite an ageless quality, an age-is-beside-the-point quality. She could be an uncommonly sophisticated twenty-five. Or an especially energetic forty. She has "been involved with wine," as she puts it, for more than a dozen years, since she was twenty, at one of her earliest restaurant gigs. She is warm but not gooey, and friendly in a no-nonsense, not obsequious way. Creeping behind her in my standard-issue New York City uniform of black dress and black leggings and boots, I feel not quite overdressed, just wrongly dressed: I thought I'd just fade into the background, but instead my formality makes me stand out a little too much. Amanda is wearing jeans and a

T-shirt and sneakers: casual, but there is no mistaking her authority and her intelligence. In less than a decade in New York City, she rose to the top of her trade.

Amanda owns strong opinions and, whereas some sommeliers might be classified as generalists, she has a distinct point of view: she's a champion of "natural wines," an imperfect but serviceable designation generally taken to mean wines to which nothing is added nor taken away during their making, and which were produced in relatively small numbers using sustainable and organic methods by independent growers from grapes that were harvested by hand. This is exactly how wine was made during most of its thousands of years in existence.

But the production of wine changed dramatically during the second half of the twentieth century, when chemical interventions, additions of natural and artificial flavors and colorants, and other "innovations" were introduced to the process, and the industry broadly became bigger, more commercial, more corporate—and less intimately bound to its sources, its makers, the challenges of soil, the caprices of climate.

Proponents of natural wines believe that wine was more interesting, more varied, and, simply, *better* before that shift occurred. (The so-called orange wine mentioned in Eater's item about the Obamas' visit to Estela refers to one category of natural wines in which white wine grapes are fermented on their skins and seeds, which impart a darker, deeper color than most white wines possess.) And if one prefers their food to be organic, untouched by pesticides and other chemicals, and produced by small farms, it follows logically that one might also favor wine that is made under similar conditions, and that meets similar criteria.

Amanda is discerning, but not snobbish, at least not in the conventional sense of the word. And if a season immersed in the world of wine has taught me anything, it's that there's a world of difference between discernment and snobbery. That distinction might just be what separates the truly great sommeliers—the ones who are more passionate than pedantic, who demonstrate taste more than rote memorization—from the lesser ones.

FAMILY MEAL IS OVER, and now Amanda makes sure that her wines by the glass are stocked. She gives me a quick tour of the tiny "cellar," which is actually upstairs from the restaurant, built into a space that also serves as a general storeroom and office—where a quick glance confirms that being a wine director easily involves as much paperwork as pleasure. Responsibilities vary from restaurant to restaurant, but, for all the romance that working with wine might suggest, rightfully or not, it's clear that a substantial part of Amanda's job is managerial. There's the invoicing, and the updating of spreadsheets. There are vendors to deal with. There's ordering. Returning. There's the regular editing and revising required by the wine list. Cellar maintenance. There's troubleshooting. Supervising. Hiring. "Organization is key," she tells me. This, she adds, "will be crushing news" to would-be sommeliers who don't already know to expect it. It's not all tasting, and talking about, beautiful wine.

I follow her back downstairs to the pass between the kitchen and the dining room, where Emily, the maître d', briefs the floor staff on the VIPs who will be dining with them that night, among other useful information she dispenses. For her part, Amanda tells the servers to "keep it tight with comps tonight." Which means: It's nice to make a customer feel special now and again, but there's no need to give too much wine away. There's friendly chatter about regulars who are getting engaged. An impromptu alliteration game involving items on the menu (it seems that most of this crew loves language—and Keara, one of the younger sommeliers, whom Amanda has mentored through stints at a few different restaurants, is also a poet). There is the usual kind of jokey banter that happens at restaurants in the liminal hour before service starts.

The chef de cuisine, Sam Lawrence, enumerates the specials and asks Amanda to chime in with pairing ideas. "Aperitivo wines are nice with crudités," she says. "The fresher the wine, the better they will show." With grilled foie gras and grape leaf, she suggests a bottle from the Pyrenees: "It's long for a rosé." That sounds exactly right to me. Foie gras and grape leaf and a long, cold glass of rosé? Yes, I'm thinking, I want *that*.

The chef tests the staff on the information he shared minutes earlier with a rapid-fire round of questions: *"What are wood ears?" "Where's the steak from?" "What kind of eggplant is it?"* They have it down. Amanda asks a few more pointed questions about the steak, and is told that it's "lacquered with garlic oil, beef fat, and fish sauce"—and it's almost like I can see her paging through the restaurant's big book of wine offerings in her mind, considering the bottles that will complement all of those big flavors. Right now, the number of bottles listed in the book hovers around 300.

Amanda carries two armloads of wine bottles over to the bar, then dashes upstairs to deal with a troublesome delivery issue. I stand beside Emily, at her maître d' station, waiting, and making small talk. I say something blandly but truthfully flattering about Amanda—along the lines of "she's really good at what she does."

Emily quickly agrees, and almost as quickly adds: "Her other calling is teaching." I'd already started to see what she means by that. "She's a history buff, and she makes it fun." Amanda is a master of precise and evocative descriptions, but her pedagogic style is Socratic: she wants and expects the sommeliers and servers with whom she works to taste and think for themselves, and to express their ideas with clarity, confidence, and conviction. (I'll see this in even fuller effect the next day—at the weekly "wine class" she conducts for the restaurant's staff.)

I'D BEEN A BARTENDER since the mid-1990s, and had only stopped very recently before the night I trailed Amanda at Estela. I am accustomed to working on my feet, but suddenly I'm not sure I'm going to survive this shift. And naturally, just as this wave of worry washes through me, it's too late to turn back. It's opening time, and the first guests have begun to file in.

It's not a mad rush, not at first. Two two-tops fill up right away. Then four people claim seats at the bar. The guests who arrive during "first turn"—not a formal, scheduled seating, but broadly the first influx of customers into the restaurant when service starts—aren't quite as serious about wine as diners in the later turns will be. The early birds are more concerned with food than drink. Still, this is a weekday evening, which, I am told, means the people who are out for dinner will probably drink more wine—and care about it more, and know it better—than their weekend counterparts.

Many of Estela's guests are epicurean tourists, people for whom eating and drinking well is the best portion of seeing the world. They're fun, they're open, they're interested in trying new things, but they can also be demanding. Guests who understand up front what kind of food and wine happen at Estela know not to expect the kinds of traditional, "prestige" bottles they might find, say, at an upscale steakhouse. They might already know that natural wines dominate the list here—and that that's an understatement, as natural wines make up the whole of the list. But, even knowing all this, there are times, Amanda says, when a guest might find a wine a little too challenging. Once in a while.

At one table for two, both of the guests have ordered beer. Amanda likes beer—and there's a fine selection of mostly local bottles at the restaurant. But it's a sign: They're scared of wine, and the thought of a conversation with a sommelier probably scares them even more. She's not going to force it on them. Even people like these, who choose to eat at a place like this, are intimidated by wine, and by the prospect of talking with a sommelier.

Then a group of young men breezes in—Wall Street types, finance dudes, bros in blazers. They're seated at a table near the back. More than a decade working as a bartender has taught me that it can only go one of two ways with guys like these: There's an excellent chance that they're going to be entitled twits who utter not a single "please" or "thank you," but there's also a possibility that they'll be polite and friendly and well brought up, in possession of impeccable manners, embodying a sort of old fashioned noblesse oblige. They start with a round of martinis.

"They'll be looking for a full-bodied red," Amanda predicts, whispering to me as we stand a few yards away from their table. The guys are not whispering, and we overhear them order almost every dish on the menu (most are suitable for sharing). Amanda riffles through the book. "Never approach a table without some ideas in mind," she tells me, before walking toward them.

She offers the guys—let's call them the Blazers—the book. It's a cue that says, "When you're ready, I'm ready."

One of them has been designated to take charge. He doesn't look completely comfortable in this role, but he is less anxious than his companions. As if on cue, he tells her they're going to want a pretty big red—but maybe they'll have a bottle of white first. She's not surprised to learn that the sort of white they want is chardonnay, a white Burgundy. And they would like it very, very cold, please.

Amanda manages to keep the whole room in her sights while tending to the Blazers, scanning to see where cocktails are finished, where glasses are low, even though she praises the servers for their adroitness and attention to detail. She watches one of them bringing the grandest glasses in the house—vessels that could comfortably accommodate a pair of goldfish—to a table, even though the wine that the host of the table has ordered does not require them for optimal enjoyment. But Amanda does not disapprove: on the contrary, she knows that the server has read his customers well. These are people who like fancy glassware, and probably fancy everything. These are people who relish, and expect, a bit of "zhuzzhing," Amanda says. Some diners like to be fussed over; others just want to be left alone. Divining their desires is a valuable skill in a sommelier, but when it's not possible, good, clear communication does the job just as well.

Meanwhile, the Blazers have been drinking, fast. Happily, they've turned out to be the rarer, better version of Wall Street dudes, all politesse and relaxed gratitude. They are loving the food. They are loving the wine. And even when they've grown a little loud (inevitable after a round of martinis and two bottles of wine) they are still disarmingly good-natured. They put their faith in Amanda not to misguide them, and she, in turn, acknowledges and appreciates their trust in her. They do not require any hard sell, but that doesn't mean that she will take advantage of their openness, or exploit their insecurity where wine is concerned. She wants them to have a great experience—and maybe learn something, too. It may sound dramatic when she says that she perceives one of her objectives as a sommelier to "open the gates of knowledge," but it's clear she sincerely means it. She wants all of her guests to learn a thing or two about wine, where it's from, and the people whose labor and skill and care bring it into existence. "When you withhold knowledge," she says, "you can really rip people off."

If the worst caricature of sommeliers portrays them as intimidating, supercilious pedants determined to upsell to customers the most expensive bottles they can (and experience tells me that this stereotype is grounded in some truth),

Amanda operates in a very different fashion. She wants you to drink something good, and she wants that something good also to be something you might not experience elsewhere, under the guidance of a different sort of sommelier. In a 2017 article for the Web magazine *SevenFiftyDaily*, she wrote:

> [W]hat's the point of being a sommelier if you're
> not doing this very thing—educating yourself about
> philosophies of viticulture and winemaking around
> the world and the changing trends in wine drinking?
> Why bother building a list if you don't love teaching
> about and sharing wine, in its remarkable diversity?
> Why stock wines that taste the same as all the other
> wines on the shelf, that provide nothing of specificity
> beyond "This one's red and that one's white"? There's
> one understanding of hospitality and wine service
> that says: Give a guest what they say they want,
> make money off it, and don't push discourse. As for
> me, I have always preferred dialogue over mute
> acquiescence.

It's as close to a manifesto as Amanda has put on paper. She knows that, as a woman, as a person in her early thir-ties, as someone who did not pursue certification or titles through any of the governing bodies that test and award credentials to sommeliers around the world, she doesn't perfectly fit the mold of what some consider the ideal of "a classical sommelier." And she will show you that that doesn't matter, because she knows who she is as a sommelier, and she knows what she wants to give to her guests.

IT'S FAR FROM A frantic night at Estela, but the restaurant is filling up. The crazy rice is very popular: I see a plate of it on almost every table. Toward the front of the room, there's another group of three men drinking martinis—but I can already tell they're not going to be as friendly or as game as the Blazers. When Amanda approaches their table, they look at her as though she has rudely intruded. She gives them the space they seem to want.

Toward the back of the room, a very different class of customer is settling in: a refined young European couple, a woman and a man. In their speech and their dress, they are confident, elegant, and understated. They have enviable posture. They've made a point of discussing the menu with their server before asking to speak with a sommelier, before even considering what they'll drink. They'll let the food lead. Amanda regards them from a distance, sizes them up, and registers that these are people who know things about food and wine.

When she determines that the time has come to approach the Europeans, it turns out that she was right: they know what they like, and they have plenty to say about it, in a flawlessly polite if somewhat aloof way. The man expresses his interest in bottles and vintages from a particular village. Amanda listens closely. Her inventory does not include anything from the place he has mentioned, but she understands the qualities for which it is known, and, by extension, she knows the style the couple is after.

Their style, which Amanda describes to me as "more classical" than many of Estela's other guests, feels slightly discordant with the restaurant's wine list. They are not the likeliest customers to be enchanted by the dry terrestrial funk of, say, a biodynamic orange wine from Abruzzo. But she is undeterred and unruffled, and right away has something in mind that she is sure they will like. Something "a bit rounder," she tells me, "not too earthy."

Minutes later, she returns to the Europeans with a bottle of red from Fixin, a small, lesser-known area of Burgundy's Côte de Nuits region, between Dijon and Gevrey-Chambertin. I watch how she holds the bottle as she conveys it to the table, with perfect, old-school formality: its base is cupped firmly in the palm of her left hand, its label faces out. Amanda pours, and the man holds up his glass, examines the color, and breathes in. This is sufficient to confirm that the wine is "correct." He does not drink; he knows it's the nose that does the work here, not the mouth. He is satisfied with Amanda's selection. She pours a glass for his companion, and then completes her pour for him.

I have observed that the Europeans are among very few people in the room who hold their glasses by their stems. I'm not a stickler for many wine-drinking rules, but not to hold one's glass by its stem is one of my pet peeves. Someone, sometime, somewhere impressed upon me the importance, when drinking something good, of holding your wineglass by its stem, and that made intuitive, perfect sense to me. Who wants to warm up a nice, cold Chablis with her body heat? Why besmirch a glass with grubby fingerprints? (Next time you're watching a movie or television show in which a supposedly sophisticated character is drinking a glass of wine, I can almost guarantee that he or she will be holding it by the bowl rather than the stem. It drives me a little nuts every single time.)

I feel silly even mentioning this to Amanda, but I do it anyway, and she laughs. It's true: Even if we've advanced beyond the orthodox notion that there are absolute right ways and absolute wrong ways of doing things, especially doing things with wine, it really *is* better to hold a glass by the stem, but very few people can be bothered with doing it that way.

"Would you ever tell a customer that they're not holding their glass in the best way?" I ask her.

"No," she answers.

As dedicated as Amanda is to the pedagogical part of her profession, and although she would correct those on staff who report to her (that's a professional obligation), she would not correct a customer. It is possible that her patrons would get even more enjoyment out of their wine if, for example, they held their glasses by the stems, but it's not enough of an issue, an error, a transgression to correct. To correct a customer, even with tenderness and diplomacy, introduces the risk of embarrassing that customer. And the possibility of embarrassment lies at the heart of the sometimes fraught relationship between guest and sommelier: it's that *don't call on me, don't call on me, don't call on me* anxiety I've witnessed at so many dinners in so many restaurants.

I asked Eric Asimov if he thinks restaurant customers are becoming more comfortable with sommeliers. "Not really," he said. "There's still a vestigial fear that you're going to be taken advantage of, or embarrass yourself. There's more than a little bit of shame involved."

On the floor, intimate human interaction is the heart of

the sommelier's work; her stewardship applies not only to bottles of wine, but to the humans who drink them and pay for them. My generally optimistic view of human nature tells me that, as with most people, restaurant customers want to have a good time: they've booked a table at Estela because they want to have a memorable and delicious dinner, not because they want to torture a waiter with complaints or confound a sommelier with outlandish requests that are impossible to satisfy.

But even with my generally optimistic view of human nature, I acknowledge that there are some difficult people in this world. Remember, I spent more than a decade working as a bartender. I felt the pressure to make a customer, say, an Old Fashioned exactly the way he liked it. But the stakes are surely even higher when you're selling bottles of wine that range from about $50 to upwards of one thousand dollars.

There are cases in which Amanda might strongly disagree with a guest—or just flat-out objectively know that he or she is wrong—but she can't really let it show. There's the kind of diner who will habitually insist that a bottle of wine is "corked"—that is, that it tastes off because it has been compromised by a tainted cork—and is usually wrong about it. (This behavior always reminds me of a certain kind of guy I always see in sports bars during the World Cup, who constantly calls "Offside!" and is also usually wrong).

This evening there's an even knottier situation. A customer has complained to Keara, one of the sommeliers whom Amanda oversees, about the wine she served him. He told her that he was sure that he had detected "brett" in the wine. "Brett" is short for *Brettanomyces*—a type of yeast that can be perceived in wine as a bad thing or as a good thing, depending on the wine, depending on the palate of the person drinking it, depending on the subjectivity of taste, depending on how one responds to a particular aromatic sensation often likened to how a barnyard smells. In this case, Amanda is certain it's not even present. But she and Keara want their customers to be pleased with the wine they're drinking. More than that, Amanda wants them to be moved by their wine. This isn't about winning, or even starting, arguments.

The Blazers are on their third bottle of wine now. They liked the first bottle of red Amanda recommended so much that they ordered a second. It's a deep and rich Saint Joseph, from France's Northern Rhone Valley region, and the guys couldn't be having a better time.

Another party of three has been seated. They are Spanish-speaking tourists, and Amanda notices that their server appears to be perplexed. She steps in to assist, speaking as much Spanish as she can. I see lots of encouraging nodding. I hear laughter. Amanda tells me that they've ordered one orange juice, one Fernet and Coke—and one kalimotxo, the Coke and red wine combo that is especially beloved by Basque teenagers (I'm a fan—don't knock it till you've tried it). If that's what they like, that's what they will have. This table won't be ordering a bottle—but they're going to have a good time.

One more party of three settles in. I think they're a family: an elderly man and woman, and their middle-aged daughter, with an unmistakable air of entitlement. They are very dressed up. They are unsmiling, and look determined to be displeased. They're not going to be any fun at all.

At the long marble bar, every seat is taken. There, in closer, more genial quarters, it seems a little easier for the guests to ask questions, to try things, to talk about wine less self-consciously than their counterparts at tables do. This is one reason I love eating at a bar when I go out: a bar invites relaxation, even a sense of community. It's okay to turn to the woman sitting beside you and ask her what's in her glass. It's less of an event to ask a bartender to describe a Blaufränkisch than it is to confer with a sommelier.

Around ten, service starts its slow descent, and my feet

are finished. Fewer than five hours on the floor at Estela with Amanda Smeltz on a relatively mellow weeknight have hit me harder than my customary seven-hour shift behind a bar—but I know that's partly because I haven't had time to catch on to the restaurant's particular rhythms, or to grasp the geography of the place well enough to navigate it efficiently. The physicality of this work reminded me very much of bartending, but there'd been much more running around, and running upstairs, and dashing back down again, than I'd anticipated. There was also the stay-out-of-everyone-else's-way dance, which proved to be an exertion in itself. I'd worn the wrong footwear for this.

Always watchful, Amanda could see how tired I was, that I was ready to call it a night. I thanked her. "I hope the rest of the night goes smoothly," I said. She seemed certain it would. "See you tomorrow in wine school." She still had hours to go before her night was over.

**2**

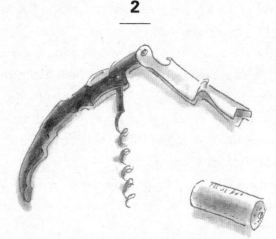

There's a reason I've never suffered from a fear of sommeliers, and his name is Roger Dagorn. In the 1990s, he was the sommelier at New York City's Chanterelle, a restaurant of the sort often forbiddingly (and annoyingly) described as "temples" or "monuments." But if the fearsome reputations of such places set up the expectation that they had to be staffed by the most exalted and priestly of professionals (I remember Bianca Bosker's tracing of the sommelier lineage back to the sacred cupbearers of ancient Egypt), the service at Chanterelle subverted that expectation. And if the office of sommelier is arguably the most hieratic of all fine-dining functionaries, its legendary sommelier is likely the friendliest and most down-to-earth sacred cupbearer you'll ever meet.

His restaurant career began when he was a teenager, at his family's French restaurant in midtown Manhattan, Le Pont Neuf. But I'll always associate him most closely with Chanterelle, where he worked from 1993 until the restaurant closed in 2009, and where he was honored with a James Beard Award for Outstanding Wine Service, and in this I don't think I'm alone. Chanterelle was an unusual place— still discussed and mourned by many a decade after it shut its doors for the last time.

Ruth Reichl, the restaurant critic for the *New York Times*, known for her democratic taste (it could be a "monument" to haute cuisine one week, a humble Chinatown noodle joint the next) granted it four stars—the highest acclaim she could bestow—in 1993. After rhapsodizing about the food and the service, this is how she concluded:

> *Leaving the restaurant late at night, you walk out into the near-silence of a deserted street. As you stand waiting for a taxi, turn back and take one last look. The people inside, caught in the shimmering golden light of the room, look blessed.*

I can attest to its specialness, too. In 1995, two years after that review was published, I knew the beatific aura, that golden shimmer, of which Reichl spoke—but not exactly firsthand: I had glimpsed it through a pub window. That year, not long out of college myself, I'd moved back home to New York City, and had taken a job teaching at a community college in Tribeca. I found a bar near the campus that was just right for grading stacks upon stacks of freshman English compositions while nursing a pint or two of Guinness. Set on the corner of Hudson Street and Harrison Street, the bar had great big windows that flooded the room with light by day, and that by night provided an excellent view of Chanterelle. The restaurant was right across Harrison Street. And Reichl was exactly right: captured in the soft light of that dining room, the people lucky enough to eat there had an almost otherworldly, sanctified glow. How I envied them.

Chanterelle seemed unattainable to a young teacher, beyond aspirational, way out of reach. Still, I'd slow down to glance at the menu whenever I walked by, and feel a faint jab of hunger mixed with desire—and I'd daydream about what it would be like when I got to have dinner there. I would start with the seafood sausage everyone talked about. There was no question that I would finish with cheeses served from the cart I'd spied through the window, gliding smoothly around the room like a friendly ghost. Of course all of this would have to be accompanied by wine. Exceptionally good wine that I absolutely could not afford, and probably never would.

TOWARD THE END OF the first semester, I'd started dating another teacher. He had grown up in the Livermore Valley, one of California's smaller wine-producing areas, and had worked at a small winery in high school. Although Frank's studio apartment was largely unburdened by material possessions other than books, he had a much better *batterie de cuisine* than most men I knew in their mid-twenties. He had a beloved, well-seasoned cast-iron skillet. And he had a wine rack.

What he didn't have were expensive clothes. Or shoes. Or haircuts. Instead, he saved up what money he could for once- or twice-yearly splurges at great restaurants. And when we met Chanterelle was at the top of his list. I don't recall what the occasion was that first emboldened us to make a reservation there. It might have been a birthday, or maybe an anniversary. But I do remember it was a big deal. After more than a year of gazing at its menu longingly, we were actually going to eat some of those dishes that had acquired nearly mythical status in our imaginations.

We were not disappointed. The kind-eyed hostess, Karen Waltuck, whose husband, David, was the chef, gave us a friendly welcome in the art-filled foyer. The dining room was serenely pretty, not flashy or overdesigned in that headache-inducing way endemic to so many restaurants. Its walls were painted in a comforting yellow-white (Reichl described it as "apricot"—but to me it looked more like thick buttercream) that I've since tried to replicate in my home, broken up by fluted wooden panels and sideboards. Flashes of color were supplied by towering, artful arrangements of fresh flowers. The high, recessed ceiling was hung with enormous brass chandeliers.

According to plan, we started with the seafood sausage. And every single bite of our entire dinner, from the sausage to the cheese, was so good that I don't remember us speaking more than a few words. But if we were asked to isolate one single detail that stood out most on a long list of delights, neither Frank nor I would have hesitated to answer: the brightest star of the evening was the sommelier, Roger Dagorn.

After we placed our dinner order, Frank, with his wine-country background, knew to ask to speak with the sommelier; I'm not sure I even knew what a sommelier was back then. An elegant, smiling man soon materialized at the side of our table. He struck me as one of those people blessed with a gift for putting others at ease (since Frank was shy by nature, I was especially grateful for this), and he radiated warmth. We told him about what we were going to eat, and then he and Frank got into the specifics about pairing.

Frank and I probably had the lowest incomes in the room, but no one made us feel like we mattered less than any of the other guests, and I'm sure there were some VIPs in our midst. Frank was, well, frank with Roger about what we could realistically spend on a bottle of wine (this, I learned from him that night, is perhaps the most important first step in an honest and productive conversation with a sommelier). He let him know that one bottle would be our maximum, so it would have to be some kind of magical shape-shifter of a wine that would complement both the seafood sausage and whatever our main courses were. Not only was Roger unfazed by our criteria and our budget, but he also chose a perfect bottle that was priced substantially south of our upper limit.

Roger took his time with us. He listened closely. And he selected for us a wine that we could afford that still made us feel special. We lingered with our one perfect bottle until it was time for cheese, and agreed we'd treat ourselves to a glass of dessert wine each, too. I'm pretty sure that was partly because we wanted another opportunity to speak with, and learn from, Roger. We knew he had other customers who needed him, but we didn't want to let him go.

I hadn't read Reichl's 1993 review when it originally appeared in the *Times*, but reading it now, more than a quarter of a century later, I'm moved by how perfectly she captures him:

> [T]he sommelier, Roger Dagorn, is there with a smile. In fact, few restaurants offer such pleasant and unintimidating wine service. Mr. Dagorn is clearly enamored of this unusual list; he has good wines at every price level, and he discusses each with deep affection. "This is a wonderful wine," he offered one night, "but a couple of bottles have been off, so please tell me if it isn't everything it should be."

So it's no wonder that I feel so fortunate that Roger Dagorn was my first sommelier, is it? I'd known nothing about his profession. I had no preconceptions, no expectations. But first impressions are powerful, and my first impression of the office of the sommelier came from Roger, who modeled not only how knowledgeable and informative a sommelier could be, but also how gracious, modest, and generous one should be. I did not know then that by the first time I met him, he had already been a sommelier for more than twenty years.

Roger Dagorn made my first experience with a sommelier so easeful and so pleasurable, I have never since felt intimidated by sommeliers, and have never hesitated to speak with them, to ask questions, to let my ignorance show. Instead, in the presence of a sommelier, I'm happy to disclose what I don't know—so that I may learn something.

But this does not mean that all sommeliers are like Roger Dagorn. In the decades between that night at Chanterelle and now, I've seen dozens of other sommeliers at work, and very few can match him for knowledge or for tableside manner. He set the bar high. The best I've encountered since then—younger sommeliers like Amanda Smeltz— invariably share his passion for his field, and his excellence at transmitting what he knows.

When Chanterelle closed in 2009, Pete Wells wrote a brief eulogy for the website of the *New York Times*. Wells recalled his first meal there, during which he joked with the waiter that he'd drink whatever he was told to drink; he didn't feel like thinking about it too hard (he may have been joking, but this reflects exactly what many diners feel when they know they're about to be presented with a wine list as long as *War and Peace*). The waiter had a sense of humor, too, and advised him never to give up his right to think for himself, lest someone take it away.

"Much of that meal is lost to me now but I remember one course clearly: a beef carpaccio with black truffles," Wells writes. "The sommelier, Roger Dagorn, poured a daiginjo sake with a mushroomy undertone. It was an uncanny choice, well worth the risk of temporarily ceding my right to think for myself."

*Uncanny* is the right word to express his ability to pair the right drink with the right food, sometimes in surprising, even daring, ways. One can learn, both from books and from experience, about certain classic combinations that are pretty much guaranteed to please: Muscadet with oysters, for example, or Sauternes with foie gras. But there is room, in the sommelier's work, for imagination, and for surprises. Even, or maybe especially, when they seem counterintuitive, strange—uncanny.

What I remember best from my *last* time at Chanterelle is that, as our dinner wound down, I asked Roger if he might recommend an Armagnac to end the night. Of course he might. But he had something else in mind. "Do you like rum?" he asked us. Sure, I liked rum. I was in my twenties. I liked all liquor. But neither Frank nor I had ever considered it an after-dinner drink, the way we thought of Armagnac or cognac or a single-malt Scotch whisky. Still, we, too, were happy to cede our right to think for ourselves to Roger, and our trust in him was rewarded.

He poured some rhum agricole—a thing we'd never heard of before—into two small snifters. It looked to me like tiger's eye quartz: deep amber, with a shimmer of dark brown. And its taste: reminiscent of cognac, but earthier. For all its refinement, a quiet but determined funkiness had found its way in, and set it apart from other nightcaps I'd known. It was an inspired choice—and it did not go unnoticed by Frank or me that it was also a less costly one than Armagnac would've been. Roger wasn't interested in selling the most expensive things in the book; he was interested in sharing his knowledge, and in introducing us to something new (to us) and beautiful. Pairing drink with food can be an act of creativity, undertaken primarily to give a diner pleasure. In his unforced, unfussy, and unfailingly warm way, Roger showed that pleasure can be enough of a virtue on its own, but it can go even deeper, by opening up possibilities and cultivating curiosity.

I followed Roger Dagorn's post-Chanterelle trajectory for a few years, until I lost his trail. Around 2013, I thought he was working at the restaurant Tocqueville, near Union

Square, when I tried to contact him for a story I was writing about rum—since it was he who had introduced me, all those years earlier, to rhum agricole. I did not hear back. I heard he was still teaching future sommeliers at the New York City College of Technology, but perhaps he was on a leave of absence when I attempted to find him there. I gleaned occasional, frequently conflicting rumors of his whereabouts—always accompanied by affectionate anecdotes. He'd gone to a fancy midtown steakhouse. He'd become a consultant. He had retired. He was making wine. He moved to France. Most of these rumors were untrue, but I gave up the hunt, and didn't pick it up again until I started working on this book, because I couldn't imagine writing about sommeliers without discussing Roger Dagorn. I had to see him again. At the very least, I wanted to thank him.

## 3

Amanda Smeltz doesn't remember ever seeing her parents, Debra and Dennis, drinking wine. We're sitting in my kitchen talking on a mild winter morning over nothing stronger than grapefruit-flavored seltzer when she tells me this, and she can see how surprised I am. "They don't drink at all, really."

She was born and raised in Harrisburg—Pennsylvania's capital city—in a working-class family. Smeltz is an old Pennsylvania Dutch (that is to say, German) name. Her father's family can trace itself back three hundred years in the region. Her mother's family's roots are Norwegian, among the many Scandinavian immigrants who settled in the Midwest and the northern states once covered with tallgrass prairie, Minnesota and Wisconsin.

Amanda's perspective on drinking differs from many other members of her immediate family. "Attitudes toward alcohol in my family are a lot more cagey—and they're a lot more frightened, for a really good reason," she explains. A history of alcoholism on her mother's side partly accounts for her parents' aversion to alcohol in every form, including wine. There's less anxiety about it on her father's side, but her paternal grandfather, whom she describes as "a loving and sweet and quiet man," drank a lot, too, like many workingmen of his generation born in the beginning of the twentieth century. In her family, Amanda says, "there's the old American association with alcohol mostly being a problem."

Given her family's history, she understands and respects why her parents don't drink. But she regrets that they never got to experience drinking as a pleasure rather than an instrument of affliction, and that they never got "to interact with wine in a way that's deeply connected to cooking." For them, food was chiefly for nourishment, and alcohol was for getting drunk; they had observed no model of a meaningful relationship between eating and drinking. There was not what Amanda identifies as a more typically European conception of a vital, complementary union between wine and food, "where you have a tumbler of white wine with lunch, and two glasses of red with pasta, and this is how we grew up on our grandfather's farm." The American mind has a different way of thinking about eating and drinking, she suggests—one that is often alienated from people and place. "That connection has been severed. I come by it through a back door, for sure."

Although her parents don't drink, their influence is nonetheless felt in the way Amanda does her job. One of her goals is to make her guests feel very much the way Roger Dagorn made me feel when I had dinner at Chanterelle: like I belonged there as much as anyone did, even if my budget was far more modest than many, if not most, of the restaurant's patrons. "When I think about where I come from, I can't ever do anything to keep people like me out. People like my parents, or like my siblings," Amanda says. "It's so easy to be intimidated by stuff that's this heavy with the trappings of class and money." Class is seldom discussed in the sphere of fashionable restaurants, a world that is often preoccupied with wealth and status and luxury, and often rigidly hierarchical.

Amanda started waitressing in high school, in what she calls the "very straightforward mom-and-pop restaurants" that are familiar in central Pennsylvania. It was when she left Harrisburg to go to college in Milwaukee (although she is not Catholic, she always wanted to go to a Jesuit school, and chose Marquette University) that she started working in fine dining. And it was in Milwaukee, a city whose identity and history are inextricably bonded to beer, whose nicknames include Beertown and Brew City, that Amanda's education in wine began in earnest.

She landed a job at a restaurant called the Mason Street Grill, in Milwaukee's venerable Pfister Hotel, a downtown landmark that opened in 1893. The restaurant is an upmarket steakhouse, exactly the sort of place where I could imagine a brewing executive and his guests digging into a porterhouse with sides of Delmonico potatoes and creamed spinach— accompanied by a $300 bottle of Napa Valley red. It's where Amanda developed an interest in and, she says, a palate for wine: "Had I not worked in restaurants, I don't know that I ever would have learned anything about it."

And her time at Mason Street gave her something equally, if not more, invaluable: her first mentor. It was Amanda's good fortune that the restaurant's manager was a man named Peter Donahue. "His career was sort of amazing," she says. "We bonded early on because he was from New York, and I had been feeling fairly isolated and out of place in Milwaukee. I felt pretty sharply the difference between mid-Atlantic, East

Coast culture, and midwestern Great Lakes culture. And then I landed this job and the general manager, the person who tended to the wine list and cellar, had lived and worked in New York City for a solid twenty years."

It wasn't just that Donahue had worked in New York City: it's *where* he worked in New York City. He had been part of the team that opened Danny Meyer's restaurant, Gramercy Tavern—which is legendary for its food, its wine, and its service. This didn't mean anything to Amanda at the time, but she came to understand it—and to understand that being trained by a Gramercy Tavern alumnus meant a lot in the world of restaurants. "It was super humane," Amanda says, describing the style of service she learned from Donahue. "It was extremely personable. It was deeply respectful. It was also really professional and very polished—without being uncomfortable."

It's evident how abundantly that approach—the "Gramercy Tavern Style" as transmitted by Peter Donahue—informed Amanda's own style as a sommelier. In "What Does Great Wine Service Look Like Today?" a 2017 article for the online drink magazine *Punch*, the wine writer Jon Bonné traces what he calls the "New Casual" style of wine service directly to Gramercy Tavern—and one of the three sommeliers featured in the story is Amanda Smeltz, during her stint at Bar Boulud that preceded her appointment at Estela and Café Altro Paradiso. "It would be hard to find a better example of the intersection of old formality and the New Casual than Amanda Smeltz," Bonné writes—and that has a ring of truth about it. But for Amanda, even the "old formality" in her style came from Donahue's mentorship in the Gramercy school of service.

It may seem counterintuitive, but some formality, applied judiciously and with a human touch, can help to put guests at ease. I'd observed this when Amanda delivered bottles to tables at Estela, their labels face-forward with perfect symmetry, held so that they'd be at eye-height with seated diners. "Even if I look really different to them, and the space is noisy, and the floors are slanted, they're at least going to get a signal that someone knows what they're doing. There's good body language. Even though the reason to hold the bottle this way is not relevant to this particular wine"—she's speaking of the Fixin she selected for the European couple at Estela that September evening—"I'm still doing it for you so you can see we know what we're doing."

Donahue's mentorship also had an impact on her process of taste formation. Few people were talking about natural wine in Milwaukee back then, but Peter was interested—even if he didn't use the exact words "natural wine." Most of his customers were interested in big American wines that were assumed to play well with steak. But he knew there was more to wine than that—and he trusted that his customers would appreciate more variety, if only it were introduced to them. "I think the first thing that he helped me do, and this was really important, was to open my eyes to how incredibly diverse the world of wine was when people were drinking in a really monolithic fashion," Amanda says.

Amanda participated in every training Donahue conducted, including those she was not required to attend. He taught her how to be a cellar hand, which is often the traditional starting point toward becoming a sommelier, much like beginning as a busser or a dishwasher is on the way to becoming a chef. "You're the one downstairs moving boxes, and you learn a lot that way as a result," she says. There, in a murky but climate-controlled sub-basement of a grand old hotel, in the cellar of the Mason Street Grill, as she studied its inventory she began to understand how to read labels, and how to interpret the various and very different regional ways of classifying wines.

And as anyone who has ever stood in a wine shop and stared in bewilderment at the kinds of confounding, complicated wine labels one sometimes encounters (often on French and German bottles) knows, this is not a small thing. Right now,

I'm looking at the label on a bottle of what I rather grandly (but with tongue in cheek) like to call my "house wine"—it's very inexpensive and I like it just fine for cooking and for drinking. All that's revealed on the front of the bottle is the name of the wine and the type of grape from which it's made. On the back, more is disclosed, but not much: now I know its vintage, its country of origin, its percentage of alcohol by volume (ABV), and who imported it.

Compare that to the labels on a bottle of fine Burgundy, which are often cluttered with text. They will tell you the year of the vintage. And the name of the producer, and the village in which the grapes were grown, and the name of the vineyard. They will tell you the wine's *Appellation d'Origine Contrôlée*, which refers both to its region or sub-region and to the standard of quality it meets, which might be Grand Cru, or Premier Cru, or Village. The label may also note who bottled the wine and where, its ABV, and, as if you couldn't tell, that it's a product of France. And all of that is probably on the labels on the front of the bottle—there's more to learn on the back.

This abundance of information is extremely helpful— if you happen to know quite a lot about Burgundian winemakers, vineyards, villages, what distinguishes a Grand Cru from a Premier Cru, and if 1987 is considered a better, or worse, year than 1989 for the wine. Otherwise, much of it is inscrutable. But a well-stocked restaurant wine cellar is a good place to start getting cozy with, and deciphering, the data. (Strangely, omitted from virtually all labels of distinguished Burgundy wines are the names of the grapes from which it's made. It's assumed that if you seek Burgundy out, you already ought to know that the white stuff is made from Chardonnay and the red from Pinot Noir.)

From Peter Donahue she also learned the systems by which a wine program operates, the primacy of organization (a trait Amanda doesn't consider an inherent personal strength but one she has had to train and cultivate for her work), the very specific spatial demands it makes. "It's a really great way to begin. I was probably twenty-one at the time. I did that for probably a year and a half and got to know the cellar really well, and the wine list inside and out."

The Mason Street Grill was the site of Amanda's earliest significant sense memories associated with wine, from which she still distinctly remembers producers, grape variety, place, and flavor—probably because it was there that she saw how she could put her gift with language to use in the service of talking about wine. "I mean, I have memories of drinking grocery store stuff before that and being curious about whether or not they were good. I remember the first time I tasted Argentine Malbec from a grocery store and thought, 'Wow, that was really something! I don't know what something is!' But now, looking back, I know it. My sense memories are of a super-oaky, rich, really extracted red wine, and I was responding to extremely concentrated, plummy purple flavors along with confectionary, like vanilla notes.

"What was becoming starkly clear to me was that I preferred drinking wine to what most of my collegiate peers were doing, which is, you know, crushing thirty-packs of Natty Ice, and I did that too. But just seeing that behavior around drinking confirmed the kinds of fears that my family had about the destructive nature of alcohol." She was seeing, at the same time, "a really negative drinking culture in college" and, at the restaurant, a very different model: "people drinking wine with their dinner," because it was pleasurable in itself—and because of its affinity with food.

That affinity was becoming clearer and more compelling to Amanda every day at Mason Street. She liked listening to Donahue and the chef talk about how a certain wine would go with a new dish on the menu, and "the very idea that that could be a thing at all" was news to her; it had never come up at her earlier restaurant jobs in Pennsylvania. At Mason Street, "the chef was talking about these things, and thinking about what was delicious with what, and that was eye opening for me." Still, the restaurant was very much a steakhouse: "You had your cuts of meat, and your composed entrée dishes. You had a selection of salads, a selection of flatbreads. There was a wood-fired oven in the kitchen. The food was perfectly lovely, and totally accessible. Because so many people ate beef, red wine was usually the thing."

But occasionally the chef would put up a special that went against the steakhouse grain, and those were the times when things got even more interesting for Amanda, that made her more curious about food, and about the ways in which wine could make a meal a fuller, more profound experience.

One chef's special in particular rises up vividly among her recollections: prawn étouffée, a dressed-up version of the Cajun/Creole classic, shrimp étouffée. Amanda loved it. "I was like, 'Oh wow, what is this?' It was very off-the-road for the restaurant. And I remember the Alsatian pinot gris that Peter paired it with that night. That was the first time I learned that heat, red pepper heat, can be well balanced by aromatic white wines with some viscosity." She hadn't experienced that firsthand before, and it was powerful, and joyful, and it made instant, perfect sense to her. "Most people don't even pay attention to white wine. This is an aromatic white wine, and it is *singing* with this spicy shrimp and sausage."

Wine was starting to creep into her life outside of work,

too. She noticed that she was starting to prefer drinking wine in her dorm room while studying or writing or listening to music to "playing Euchre for four hours while crushing gin and orange juice. I enjoyed both things and I did both," she remembers, "but I was beginning to see that the pleasure in drinking for me often happened in a more reflective way. And I was immediately teased by all of my peers!"

I'm quickly forming a mental picture of college Amanda: a young poet, a philosophy student, drinking good red wine, "listening to a lot of Latin American music at the time and also Japanese techno." I conjecture that she must have seemed like an alarming sophisticate to some of the people around her at the time, and she corrects me. "No, not alarming. Just annoying. Okay, pretentious." I cut her some slack: there's no better time to be pretentious than college, to get it out of one's system. But to her, the word *pretentious* is loaded, because there's a pervasive attitude that wine itself is inherently pretentious.

It occurs to me during this conversation with a sommelier who is also a poet that there's an equally pervasive attitude toward poetry. Since the night I trailed Amanda, I'd been thinking about connections between poetry and wine, how both of these ancient cultural productions came to be regarded (in twenty-first-century America, anyway) as elitist and esoteric. I'd been thinking about all the people whom I've heard say they don't like poetry—and about, how, if I probe a bit, and extract more information, what I often learn is that they trace their contempt for poetry back to one bad teacher. With wine, is it possible that one bad, snobbish sommelier, or a supercilious shopkeeper, could have the same effect?

Even Amanda, for all of her searching scholarliness, had had this kind of experience—but with science. "I always thought that I was bad at it," she says. Growing up, she had literature and history teachers who got her excited about the humanities, but the same was not true of her science teachers. Wine, which arguably brings together art and science with both intimacy and necessity, became the science teacher Amanda hadn't had before, and sparked her interest in biology and chemistry and geophysics.

When Amanda took that job at the Mason Street Grill as a college student, it was just that: a job. She did not foresee how much she would learn there, how much it would reshape her passions and priorities, and how much it would define and determine her career path. She continued working there for a year after graduation, while she considered her future in other ways: Did a poet need to go to graduate school? And if so, could she realistically afford it? As a member of the first generation in her family to go to college, and already carrying debt from her undergraduate liberal arts degree, she was beset by uncertainty. "Was this something I should even be considering at all? Was it a radically irresponsible thing for me to do?"

While she grappled with these difficult questions, she continued to learn about wine and food, and to grow into her own authority. In Milwaukee, circumstances and timing matched Amanda with a generous and encouraging mentor in Peter Donahue, who recognized her diligence and skill, and actively cultivated and encouraged them. His excellence as a mentor also came with the gloss and sparkle of years of experience in New York City—a city Amanda had always loved, and one she had visited often while she was growing up not too far away in Pennsylvania. From the time she was only fifteen, she'd had a feeling she'd live there someday. Donahue's stories galvanized that longing. And now, more than a year after finishing college in Beer City, whether she went to graduate school or not, it was obvious to her what her next stop would be.

## 4

At twenty-four, Amanda moved to New York City. She had received a solid scholarship offer from the New School University, which helped to mitigate, though not vanquish, her concerns about money and about the practicality of going to graduate school. In the autumn of 2009, she began her coursework as a master's degree student in creative writing.

Even though the costs of grad school were now more accessible to her, there was no question that she would still have to find a full-time job, and somehow fit it into or around her full-time poetry studies. With her experience, and a reference from Peter Donahue, it wasn't hard for her to find work in a New York restaurant. She took a job at a brand-new place called the Breslin, in the Ace Hotel. The English chef April Bloomfield, whose Greenwich Village gastropub the Spotted Pig had already made her a celebrity, was in charge. The Breslin would be Bloomfield's fine dining showcase. A year later, also in the Ace, Bloomfield would open the John Dory, which would, as its name suggests, focus on fish. Amanda would be part of the team that opened both.

Carla Rzeszewski was appointed wine director. It was a big job: both restaurants were smash hits from the get-go. Amanda was waiting tables. One day, not long after the Breslin opened, she overheard Rzeszewski in a meeting with the director of operations, saying that she needed an assistant. "I just happened to hear it and kind of popped my head over and said, 'I've done wine stuff in restaurants before. If you want an assistant, I could probably do it.'" They agreed to let her give it a shot.

It was exciting, being at the Breslin and the John Dory from day one. But opening a restaurant (or two) presents distinct challenges. "Oh my God, opening is the stupidest thing," Amanda says. "It's chaos. The systems aren't clear, the staffing isn't clear." Those who are hired early on in the process haven't yet revealed their strengths and weaknesses. People whom a chef or owner might've thought would make great managers turn out not to be great managers. Someone hired for the front of house turns out to have a much better disposition for the kitchen. "So there's usually a lot of rotation and movement. It's easier to walk into a system that's already in place. You can be like, okay, I'd like to rearrange this and that, but I don't have to do that right away. It's very much a hermit crab type thing. The shell is already here. I'm just going to crawl in and eventually make it mine." In a brand-new restaurant, you have to build your own shell.

She worked with Carla Rzeszewski until the spring of 2012—about two and a half years, the whole time she was completing her MFA. She remembers those years as "super tumultuous. Doing full-time graduate work in something as visceral as creative writing, while working as a somm in an extremely popular restaurant group: it was a lot of stuff to do at once."

She completed her master's thesis, which would form the foundation (about two-thirds) of her first book, *Imperial Bender*, and earned her degree. Even while working full-time at two hectic restaurants, Amanda had thrived at the New School, made some of her best friends there, and was more than satisfied with what she got out of the program. Just as it did for many of her classmates, teaching creative writing felt like the logical next step for Amanda—except that it wasn't. She watched one school friend after another apply for full-time jobs in academia's severely tight market. Many wound up as adjuncts instead, without essential benefits like health insurance, without job security, and sometimes, in a city as expensive to live in as New York City, without enough income to cover their basic bills. She witnessed some of the most talented poets and teachers she knew struggling to get jobs. "There's nothing I like better than being in the classroom," she says, and I already knew this from sitting in on just one of her wine classes at Estela. I think back to what Emily, the maître d' at Estela, told me the night I trailed: that teaching is as much Amanda's calling as wine is. If there is such a thing as a natural teacher, she is it—but she's also a pro. She has an unusual way of connecting with people and making lessons exciting, and she has the knowledge her students need. "It's the place where I'm the happiest, and I almost don't care what the subject is." In a poem called "Letter to Denny from Brooklyn," she wrote:

> I'm still working with wine,
> though the work brings less pleasure than ranting
> to undergrads about the breakdown of genre, the
>     campaign of '68.

But even if we are to assume that the narrator of the poem is a stand-in for Amanda, and that she would rather rant at undergrads than work with wine, she didn't want to subject herself to the pressures and miseries of adjunct life. She also didn't want to pack up her life and move anywhere in the country where a full-time teaching job might exist. She understood that even if the day might come when she'd no longer work in restaurants, work she'd done since she was in high school, that time had not yet arrived.

Many years after she wrote "Letter to Denny from Brooklyn," Amanda says it's no longer true that she'd rather be teaching undergrads than being a sommelier. But back then, she wrestled. "And I still worry about the how it's taking a toll on my writing life. Because the hours are brutal." Amanda estimates that she normally works fifty to sixty hours a week. "But when I look at some of my peers, who I went to graduate school with, they've also struggled with work. I think it's common for lots of creative people. It's hard to find your way in terms of what you do for pay." Her work is often exhausting, and doesn't allow for as much writing time as she'd like—but she genuinely enjoys it. She knows plenty of people who don't feel that way about what they do. "It's a really interesting way of life. This might be a devil's bargain, but it's one I'm willing to make if it means that I'm going to be mentally and emotionally stimulated. It's just tiring. Most days I'm very happy to go to work. I just sort of wish I could cook at home more, and sleep more, and wake up with the sun more. I miss that."

After finishing school and leaving the Ace, she did try something different: California. She hadn't moved to San Francisco to immerse herself in its celebrated food and wine culture. She hadn't lined up a gig at Chez Panisse or Zuni. She'd gone to the Bay Area because she was, in her words, "chasing a boy."

But before she'd left New York, she'd taken a meeting with a manager at a little upstart of a restaurant called Roberta's, on a scraggly, unlikely patch of pavement in Bushwick, Brooklyn. She had heard through her friend Max, a chef there, that they were looking for people, and that their inaugural wine director had either quit or been fired. Amanda was still set on going to California, but she liked what she heard at the meeting.

She liked the feeling of the place, and quickly comprehended and connected with its DIY, punk sensibility. The manager asked her how long she planned to be in California. She told him she didn't know. Maybe just the summer. Maybe longer.

"I'll tell you what," she remembers him saying. "Let us know when you're back in town. If Max thinks you're the real deal, I believe it. But it may be the case that we find somebody while you're away." She understood that, and promised she'd be back in touch when, and if, she returned to New York. But she was definitely interested—she filed the meeting in the back of her mind, but not too far back.

Six months later, Amanda flew back to New York City to stay, and by then Roberta's had established itself as the hippest place to eat in all of New York City, really without contest; even intractable Manhattan-centric snobs who never deigned to cross the East River somehow managed to find their way to Bushwick—a scruffier and more distant precinct than the so-called "Brownstone Brooklyn" composed of affluent neighborhoods like Brooklyn Heights and Park Slope, with which people in their demographic would have been more familiar. Roberta's attracted media attention when Bill, Hillary, and Chelsea Clinton made a pilgrimage there for pizza in 2012. (The Clintons would later visit Estela, too—but hey, that's in Manhattan.)

Like many New York lifers, I can be skeptical if not quite jaded, and the hype alone made me suspicious of this whole Roberta's business. Plus, please don't throw things at me, I'm largely ambivalent about pizza. It's fine—but not what I'd request for my final meal, if given the choice. Could any pizza, I wondered, really be worth a schlep on the godforsaken G train (widely regarded as one of the Metropolitan

Transit Authority's greatest indignities on tracks—slow and infrequent and furnished with few points from which to transfer from other subways), and then having to eat it in what looked like an oversize lean-to while sitting on a rickety, backless bench?

The answer, I discovered on my first visit, was a resounding yes. I was almost ashamed of how quickly the food made me a convert. And I even liked the ambience, which is as far removed from a place like Chanterelle as I can conjure. What Roberta's might have lacked in conventional comfort, it compensated for in fun, palpable energy. I had to concede that these hipsters, with their delicious food, were okay by me.

It was late autumn when Amanda returned to the restaurant for her second meeting, and they still hadn't hired a wine director—an unusual state of affairs. "And looking back on it, that should have been a huge red flag," she says, "because nine months without a wine director at a very popular and very busy restaurant is a bad idea. You have to have somebody there to tend the wine list. So they had been kind of cobbling it together with sticks and glue and the general manager was trying to keep it afloat."

At that second meeting, she met the owners. They had just launched Roberta's sister, Blanca, a tasting-menu-only restaurant. If Amanda was hired, both would be her responsibility. She was still intrigued. She knew she could handle it. More than that, she knew she was exactly the right person for the job. "What they wanted was for their wine program to be like the rest of their environment. *I know how to do this*," she thought, "*I'm your demographic. I can do it for you.*"

She wrote them a letter, outlining what she thought they needed. "These were rough-and-tumble dudes who were in way over their heads in some ways. They were punk dudes who were finding out that, as they hired more and more chefs and front-of-house people, the restaurant was professionalizing before their eyes, and they didn't know what to do about it." They were impressed with Amanda's letter, and made her an offer. "It was vastly under what I was worth, but I was like, you know what? Fuck it. I'm going to do it anyway."

Even if the pay wasn't great at first, it was still a step up professionally. At the Breslin and the John Dory, Amanda had been a sommelier. She had not been single-handedly responsible for ordering, for inventory, for creating and maintaining the list. At Roberta's and Blanca, she would be the wine director. The cellar would be her responsibility. It would be on her to establish and cultivate relationships with winemakers and their representatives. She would be in charge—and that prospect was both exhilarating and a little scary.

She had learned a lot at the two restaurants at the Ace, and was confident that she could do the work. Still, she could have used more guidance with the financial and organizational part of the job. "I teach people how to do this now. I focus on systemic stuff first. I always say: the wine will come, but you need to know how to organize the business side or you're going to be inefficient and you're not going to meet the financial goals that your company wants you to meet." She encourages the sommeliers she mentors to master the practical parts of the job first—and then to go wild.

Roberta's and Blanca were the first restaurants in which responsibility for hiring, training, and mentoring aspiring sommeliers fell largely to Amanda, even though she was still only in her mid-twenties herself. When I ask her what she looks for when she's hiring, the first thing that comes to her mind—and it comes very quickly, almost instantaneously— isn't taste, or credentials, or knowledge. It's ethics.

"Ethics," she says again, for emphasis. "It's going to sound silly or cheesy, but if they don't feel like a decent and a humble human being, to me wine is the wrong field. It's the wrong field because, just like in fine art—being a curator or an auctioneer—you have to have a very specialized body of knowledge that some people put a very high price on. There is a profound temptation to floof your own ego, and to imagine yourself as a sort of special, rare creature because the content of your job is so specialized. There's a temptation to think that you're more important than you are, and I think a lot of people who end up doing wine programs in impressive formal restaurants, where there's multimillion-dollar cellars, fall into this trap."

She has much more to say about why these qualities— ethics, decency, and humility—matter so much. As a sommelier, she continues, "all you are is a caretaker for other people's labor. That's *other people's* labor. You didn't make it. You didn't bottle it. You didn't ship it. You didn't drive it here. There's a humility when you remember that you're the caretaker and curator of other people's labor. And when you're presenting their labor to people who are about to consume it, I require humility." Just thinking wine is cool isn't enough; the people Amanda hires and trains must be mindful of where it comes from, and mindful of those whose work makes the pleasure of drinking it possible.

ALTHOUGH AMANDA'S INTEREST IN natural wines stretches all the way back to her days at the Mason Street Grill in Milwaukee, and deepened during her stint at the Breslin and the John Dory, it intensified at Roberta's and

Blanca. She decided that, over time, she would build an all-natural list at those restaurants. Beyond the ethics and ethos of natural winemaking, taste was her primary consideration. She took "all the industrial stuff that I just don't think tastes good" out of the cellar and off the list, as well as some of the more traditional styles of Italian red wine that were conventionally produced. "I just got rid of them. So quietly I didn't tell anyone what I was doing. I said, 'I'm just going to go ahead and do this.' No one at the restaurant group knew anything about wine. I was walking at Ground Zero." In selecting the wines she would sell and serve at Roberta's, she curated a list that was both a declaration of her individual taste and also very much in line with the restaurant's style and tone.

A glowing review by Sam Sifton in the *New York Times* in 2011 (among other things, he called Roberta's "a rural-urban-hippie-punk food Utopia," and an "unlikely cathedral to such culinary excellence") and the joint really blew up. "All of a sudden you've got people from all over the country coming to this restaurant wanting to drink wine, which means I have a captive audience," Amanda says. The restaurant was doing two hundred covers a night, bustling. "The food is already really positive. So you've got people in a good place. And the environment is already challenging, so you can break down some boundaries. I was like, 'Fuck it. This is a rare restaurant opportunity where I could do anything I want.'" Her bosses only imposed one restriction: no expensive wine. For all of its aching hipness, a meal at Roberta's cost considerably less than one at a comparably trendy uptown restaurant, and it was important that the wine list reflected that.

That was more than fine with Amanda. "I don't want to get too didactic with this stuff. I mean, all of us are walking in blood. It's hard to figure out a way to serve wine in the global capital of money without knowing that you're doing damage somewhere." These ideas are seldom given voice in fine dining, and Amanda is well aware of this, and knows that even if she's not utterly alone in her views, they do set her apart.

Her mind rumbled with questions and possibilities. "How can I push back against a culture of incredible opulence and unchecked luxury? What can I do to bring this back down to planet Earth?" she wondered. How could she make it possible for the young people she knew in Bushwick, the "normal rough kids" on skateboards, to want to drink a real bottle of Sangiovese? "How can I do that for them? How can I show them the unadulterated, unfucked-with wines that people made in Europe for centuries before the advent of industrial farming and chemical farming, which is really recent in global history, only seventy years old?"

In thinking hard about these bracing questions, and answering them, Amanda both sealed and broadcast her point of view—and, almost as a side effect, grew her reputation. Her work at Roberta's, in her first leadership role, announced to the restaurant community exactly who she was, and what she loved about wine.

"I was becoming very aware of the type of stuff that I liked and cared for. And I was also realizing that I have a fairly subversive streak, and understanding that the wine world is a place where you can push against a lot of suppositions," Amanda remembers. "The big surprise for me during those years at Roberta's was that if you have a vision and some ideas, and you know how to make a thing that reflects that vision and those ideas, people really respond to it. They're not just looking for wine. They want to be shown something."

## 5

Roger Dagorn's professional path was very different from Amanda Smeltz's. His perspective on wine also differs from hers in some essential ways: it is more general, and less ideological. But they both became, in different decades, admired and trusted leaders in their field, both resounding successes as sommeliers. I'd come to understand how Amanda got there. I had read a little about how Roger did, gleaning information wherever I could find it. But I wanted to hear more in his own words. And, besides that, I really wanted to see him again. It had been a long time. Too long.

I remember this episode of a daytime TV talk show I

watched a long time ago that was devoted to reuniting grown adults with their favorite elementary or middle school teachers—the ones who changed their lives, the ones who set them on the right track, or who introduced them to the art or science that would become their passion and livelihood. I felt something like the excitement those former students must have felt one afternoon last autumn when I was scheduled to meet up with Roger, whom I had not seen since 2009, the year that Chanterelle, the restaurant with which I think it is fair to say he is most closely associated, closed.

I think it's also fair to say that he is regarded as one of the country's greatest sommeliers, ever. Something strange and wonderful happens every single time I mention him to anyone who ever had the pleasure of meeting him, talking about wine with him, and, maybe best of all, being served wine by him. It's as though just thinking about Roger is soothing and comforting. His exhaustive knowledge of wine and spirits is one thing. But it's his kindness and easygoing charm that make people love him even more.

But let's look at the credentials. He has worked at some of New York's best restaurants. He is a former president of the Sommelier Society. He is a veteran wine educator. He has been honored by the James Beard Foundation. As of this writing, he is one of 255 Master Sommeliers certified by the Court of Master Sommeliers—theirs are the grueling examinations featured in the book *Cork Dork* and the *Somm* documentaries—in the world; the first successfully completed examination was administered in 1969. The particular merits of the CMS program are debatable, but there is no question that those who earn its Master Sommelier diploma take wine very seriously, study it with devotion and concentration, and know it very well. He's also one of an even smaller company in America of "Sake Samurai," an award bestowed by the Japan Sake Brewers Association.

But to say that Roger is not active in the dark arts of self-promotion would be an understatement: it was harder to track him down than I'd anticipated. I called and emailed some of the most well-connected and in-the-know people with whom I'm acquainted in New York's restaurant and food-writing circles, and, although every single one of them spoke of him with admiration and affection, no one seemed to know where he'd gone off to now.

He's not racking up followers on Instagram, where he has a page but has posted nothing. There is an entity called Roger Dagorn on Twitter, but with no profile picture, no tweets, no nothing, I cannot say if it is "my" Roger Dagorn. I did, however, discover that someone (not Roger himself) set up a Facebook fan page for him, so I clicked on the page's "send a message" button, sent a short message, and shrugged. The page offers little in the way of information or commentary, its most recent post dated to 2016, and it appeared to be monitored only sporadically and by whom, I do not know.

To my astonishment and joy, my message did find its way to Roger, and, some weeks after I'd written to him, he sent a nice note back to me by email, and we made a plan. When he suggested that I choose the venue, I was seized by anxiety. If I picked a restaurant, would it be good enough for him? Would the wine list be okay? Could the service possibly meet his standards?

But my temporary panic subsided when I remembered that the main reason I wanted to see Roger Dagorn again had little to do with all of his accolades. To me the main thing was that I recalled him as being one the kindest and most effortlessly gracious humans I've ever encountered. Now I felt a little ridiculous, having harbored even some fleeting anxiety at the prospect of displeasing the sommelier who showed me I didn't have to feel anxious around sommeliers. The Roger I remembered would want me to relax, and enjoy myself.

I am neurotically punctual for meetings and appointments, as though the universe might cease to exist if I materialize three minutes past the scheduled time. I showed up at Via Carota, the restaurant I'd chosen, one of my favorites, with which Roger would surely find no fault, at least none that he would mention, about five minutes early; there was no way I was going to be late to meet Roger even by a second. Still, he had beaten me there. He seems to be, at least in this way, like me—not that I'm saying he's neurotic like me, only that he, too, is not inclined to waste other people's time. He was seated at a small table waiting patiently, and he looked exactly as I remembered him from nearly a decade earlier: Beautifully dressed in a suit and tie, his beard neatly trimmed (if perhaps a bit whiter now than it was then), his face was still illuminated by the warmth I'd felt in his presence a lifetime ago, when I first met him at Chanterelle.

His story is so different from Amanda Smeltz's story, which had been so much on my mind in the weeks leading up to this reunion with Roger. Amanda had no recollections whatsoever of her parents drinking wine, or anything else. Roger's childhood was a full immersion in the culture of wine and food.

Roger was born in 1949 in Élliant, a small village in Brittany, but was only an infant when his parents moved their young family to New York. His father, Jean, a restaurateur and sommelier, opened Le Pont Neuf in midtown Manhattan (with his cousin Jean Jouas) when Roger was a teenager. His mother, Angèle, worked the restaurant's coat-check room. At age sixteen Roger started learning the ropes of the family business, and he worked in various capacities in Le Pont Neuf's dining room part-time through high school and college. Back then, Roger recalls, "much of the service was involved with tableside fileting and carving and flambéing," all of which he learned, and which now seem to be almost lost arts.

Jean Dagorn was ahead of his time in an era when few New Yorkers had any idea what a sommelier was. (As a reminder of how far we've arguably come in our knowledge of wine, the wine list for the venerable and eternally expensive Tavern on the Green from the decade before Le Pont Neuf opened includes only about twenty options—ten of which are for champagne, including four dubiously designated domestic "Champagnes.") He organized "winemakers dinners" at the restaurant, providing a showcase not just for wines, but for the people who made them. The restaurant attracted customers who loved good, classic French food, and who appreciated French wine.

More than three years after Le Pont Neuf closed, some of its devoted regulars arranged a reunion dinner, at which the cousins Jean Dagorn and Jean Jouas were the guests of honor. The feast was covered by the *New York Times*, and one of the regulars interviewed for the story, Linda German, attested to the restaurant's unusual character:

> One of the particularly pleasant things Mrs. German recalled was the "captain's table." "If you came in alone, they'd often put you with other people who came in alone that they thought you would like," she said. "And they were always introducing their customers to one another. That's how we got to know each other."
>
> "We had wine-tasting dinners, and game dinners in the fall, and they even organized trips to France," she said. "I went on one. It was wonderful."

In anecdotes like these, one can practically feel the camaraderie and the fun, and envision the lively dinners, the plates of pheasant or quail or venison. But this struck me as even more remarkable:

> [Mrs. German] recalled, too, that when Mr. Dagorn's late wife became ill, the regulars volunteered as blood donors to give 50 pints of blood. Penelope Karageorge . . . one of the reunion's organizers, said there was another side to the coin. "If you didn't come in for a while, one of them would telephone, not to

> *hustle business, but to find out if everything was all*
> *right," she said.*
>
> *[. . .] "It was a community," Miss Karageorge said.*
> *"There was an extraordinary amount of love and*
> *caring and compassion."*

How often does one read words like "love and caring and compassion" when reading about a restaurant? Who wouldn't be moved by these poignant, intimate accounts of a restaurant whose owners treated their customers like family, and who were treated like family by them in return? It makes perfect sense that Roger Dagorn emerged from an environment like this, and he has carried these traits, learned and lived and nurtured in the family business, with him throughout his career in hospitality.

The stories about Le Pont Neuf sound more like the kind one hears about cherished neighborhood bars—acknowledged as "third spaces" beyond home and office that function as sources of community—than the stories one usually hears about restaurants, no matter how beloved some restaurants are.

Two restaurants as different as Le Pont Neuf, which served classic French food and wine in midtown Manhattan in the 1960s and 1970s, and Roberta's, which continues to offer pizza and natural wine to Brooklyn hipsters and those who wish to eat like them, if only for a night, were committed to cultivating a sense of community. At their best, both strove to go beyond the realm of the purely transactional, and succeeded at it.

Nevertheless, neither Amanda nor Roger would dispute the charge that a significant part of a sommelier's job is to be, well, transactional. Selling wine to customers is self-evidently central to what they have to do. But both see themselves, rightly, as more than mere salespeople. Both are aware of the tenacious perception that sommeliers habitually, even gleefully, upsell—and both have sold a great deal of wine, sometimes very expensive wine, in their careers without conforming to this stereotype. For most customers, even discussing money creates discomfort; it's another aspect of the guest-sommelier relationship that presents the potential for embarrassment, and another opportunity for a sommelier to put a guest at ease. The clearer both parties are from the start of their conversation, the less fraught the transaction will be.

Roger pointed out to me that the pressure to upsell often originates in working on commission—"the more they sell, the more they make"—which he has never done. "I've never had the pressure to upsell." He doesn't believe it's the best way to approach wine, or to approach people. "That's not the right reason to be in the dining room. It should be fun for the customer, and fun for yourself. The fun is in the conversation: 'That's a good wine—but I have something better, and it's less expensive.'"

Aside from its self-evident pleasures—the professional obligation to taste a lot of wine, the fun to be had in sharing one's passion and enthusiasm, the camaraderie of restaurant work, and the excellent travel opportunities—being a sommelier can also, in a very practical sense, be a good way to make a living. According to a 2017 survey conducted by GuildSomm (an international nonprofit membership organization for sommeliers and other wine industry professionals), the median annual income for responding sommeliers was $62,000. For wine directors, it was $76,000. And for those with Master Sommelier certification from the Court of Master Sommeliers, it was a robust $164,000.

ROGER STUDIED GEOLOGY AT New York City's Queens College, from which he graduated in 1972. He was offered a job related to his field of study, working in the oil business in Louisiana. But he thought about it, and decided not to take it. Instead, like many young people of his generation, he hit the road and traveled across the country. When he got to California, he visited the winemaker Joseph Heitz in Napa, whom he had gotten to know at the winemakers' dinners his father organized at Le Pont Neuf.

Joe, as he was called by almost everyone, was a towering and influential figure in California winemaking. He'd come to the business by chance during World War II when he was stationed near Fresno on an air force base where he served as a mechanic. Looking to pick up a little pocket money, he found extra work at the Italian Swiss Colony winery (now defunct, but it had once been the state's leading wine producer). The course of his career and life were changed forever—and so too was California's winemaking culture.

Joe went on to study winemaking at one of the discipline's major institutions, the University of California, Davis, made wine at Gallo and Beaulieu, and taught at Fresno State University. And then, in 1961, he bought his first vineyard, an eight-acre plot near St. Helena, for $5,000. During his lifetime, he would eventually own 350 acres planted with grapes.

Temperamentally and physically, Joe, who died in 2000, sounds like Roger Dagorn's opposite: In one obituary, he was described as "[t]all, intense, and with some irascible," and in another, in his local paper, the *Napa Valley Register*, he was characterized as "salty." But Roger speaks of him with fondness and gratitude. "He was a perfectionist," Roger says.

During that visit to Napa in the early 1970s, the young man and the winemaker talked about soil, vines, and grapes—the things that make up the foundation of a real understanding of wine. It can be easy to forget that wine is an agricultural product, and that its production and quality are powerfully influenced, if not absolutely determined, by the same factors that affect crops and farmers of all kinds. Seeing this on a visit to a vineyard brings the connections between wine and soil, wine and weather, vividly to life. Even for someone like Roger, who already loved wine, it deepened his respect for it. And it wasn't just about the liquid in the bottles. He liked the theory. He liked the science of viticulture. And, perhaps most of all, he liked the people who made it. "That's where the quality of the wine comes from. That's something I teach my students to this day," he says.

"As much as I learned in college," Roger remembers, "I learned more in one day with Joe Heitz." If he needed any confirmation that the oil business wasn't for him, that was it. (In his classes at the New York City College of Technology, a winery visit is a requirement.)

When he returned home to New York with a much clearer sense of what he wanted to do with the rest of his life, he continued to work at Le Pont Neuf, and enrolled in a sommelier training course, from which he graduated first in his class, just as his father had before him. But if an abiding love for wine and food and hospitality was part of his inheritance from his Breton father, and from the French restaurant in which he grew up, it didn't mean that Roger could coast, or that he inherently possessed the knowledge that working closely and deeply with wine demands. He studied hard. "I frequently read until four in the morning," he says. "I took very good notes."

Roger took his first official sommelier position at the restaurant Maurice, in the Parker Meridien hotel, where he remained for eight years, for most of the 1980s. During that time, he started training for and entering sommelier competitions. He quickly racked up awards, including Best Sommelier in New York City in the food and drink communications and marketing agency Sopexa's competition, and, twice in a row, first runner-up in nationals. It might shock anyone who's ever been served wine by Roger to learn that he passed the theory and blind-tasting portions in his first attempt at the Court of Master Sommeliers exams—but failed service. He's philosophic about it: "If you don't make mistakes, you'll never learn." He retook that part of the exam six months later, and passed. He had studied hard for the tests. He took them seriously. These honors and distinctions "felt good," Roger says, and it's possible that they opened some restaurant doors for him, but he doesn't dwell on them. "You can learn a lot" from studying for, and taking, the CMS test, "but you can be a great sommelier without it."

He believes that anyone can learn proper service: He has taught countless students how to serve wine, and it's a skill, like most, that improves with experience. And, while his years of experience and his status as Master Sommelier confirm that he is excellent at blind tasting—that thing sommeliers and other wine aficionados can do that most reliably dazzles laypeople—he does not venerate the practice. "One day you can nail a wine," he says, "and the next day you miss it."

Are there people, I ask him, "who just have really good taste?"

"No." His answer surprises me. "You have to work at it." He refuses to acknowledge the possibility that his palate is better than anyone else's. And he tells me this with certainty, looking me right in the eyes. I don't know if I'm convinced. But I know that he is.

Roger's primary study partner for the CMS test and other competitions was Larry Stone, whom he describes as a "brilliant fellow." Roger was in New York, Larry was in Seattle, and they spent hours on the phone, discussing the oenological arcana they were determined to master, and testing one another. Larry is another legend in the wine world, esteemed for his intellect (he was a Fulbright Scholar in comparative literature at Germany's University of Tübingen), his work ethic, his humility, and his generosity. He served as sommelier at restaurants including Charlie Trotter's in Chicago, and Rubicon in San Francisco. He retired from restaurant work in 2006 and went to work right at the source, managing wineries in California and then Oregon. Today Stone owns and operates a winery of his own, Lingua Franca Wines, in Oregon's Willamette Valley.

Intensive studying together brought them close, and Dagorn and Stone remain friends. They sound like kindred spirits, who share the same ethos and approach with respect to the work of the sommelier. In a 2017 interview with Katherine Cole for *SevenFiftyDaily*, Larry Stone said bluntly that people who don't like being on the floor shouldn't be sommeliers. "A sommelier really needs to connect in a way that is very simple," he told Cole. "Most people coming to the restaurant know nothing about wine and in fact are probably intimidated by you." Like Roger, he sees putting people at ease, and sparing them any embarrassment, as part of the sommelier's job.

Even when they met, as young men, both knew a lot about wine. But each was able to fill in whatever gaps the other had, and to ask good questions. They educated and encouraged one another, and both became stars in their field. When Roger describes his friendship with Larry, it sounds almost paradoxical: a mentorship of equals.

AFTER HIS TENURE AT Maurice, Roger's next stop as sommelier was at a stylish Chinese restaurant called Tse Yang, which had an impressive selection of wines and spirits already in place when he arrived there, and where he was given free rein to expand its list (within reasonable limits, as its cellar was small). After years of pairing wines with French, or distinctly French-inflected, food, he relished the challenge posed by having to consider which wines would best accompany the flavors of Tse Yang's beautifully executed Chinese dishes. "It was a lot of fun," he says. "A beautiful dining room. Nice people. And we sold good wines."

He worked at Tse Yang for two separate stints: between the first and the second, he got his feet wet as a teacher.

Roger's teaching career began at the French Culinary Institute, now known as the International Culinary Center (he still lectures there). He taught classes on cheese and wine, and managed the dining room, L'École, a kind of laboratory-as-restaurant in which student chefs cooked for paying guests, and student sommeliers helped those guests select wines.

Tuition for its ten-week intensive sommelier training program now runs close to ten thousand dollars. The New York City College of Technology, where Roger has taught for twenty years, is a different kind of institution: a public college, part of the City University of New York, that grants both associate's and bachelor's degrees in hospitality management. For in-state students, the tuition is around $3,500 per semester, each of which is roughly fifteen weeks. The comparison isn't a perfectly fair one: students might be drawn to ICC because there they can focus exclusively on wine, without having to fulfill distribution requirements, without having to study anything but wine, without the expectations that come with earning a college degree. For some aspiring sommeliers, compared to paying for the usual four years of college it takes to complete a bachelor's degree, the investment of time and money in a ten-week course might make more sense. But I doubt that any educational institution can compare to CUNY for diversity, and this includes attracting students from working-class backgrounds.

At City Tech, Roger says, he's had many students who never even tried a sip of wine before taking his introductory class. And in that class, "amazing things happen." For his students, as for his restaurant customers, Roger likes to demystify wine—without ever stripping it of its spirit. In some ways, he say, "students who haven't tasted anything before are easier to teach to focus" than those who have more experience tasting. And focus is everything: As long as students focus, they can do this. They can be taught how to smell. They can be taught how to taste. And from these, they learn how to identify—and, eventually, to blind taste correctly.

"It's not about luck," Roger says, or taste. It's about paying close attention, and doing the work. For extra credit, the students in his introductory class are given a glass of wine to analyze. They must identify the grape, the country of origin, the appellation, and the vintage. Each semester, two or three students out of twenty-five "nail it," he says, which is pretty respectable for students who came in knowing nothing, or next to nothing, about wine.

It's hard not to think of Amanda Smeltz as I listen to Roger speak about his students. At the beginning of her professional life, by her own admission she knew nothing about wine. She had not grown up with it. She had not yet studied it. But with a great mentor and a powerful work ethic, she became not only an expert, but an advocate. And when Roger adds that "stories are good" when talking to customers about wines, I can't help thinking how much he would've enjoyed hearing Amanda talk about Johannes and Erich Weber's wines of wind and rock, about their cold and wild and beautiful patch of land in the Mosel valley.

It isn't enough for him, either, that someone who wants to be a sommelier thinks wine is cool—he wants to know what drives a person's interest in it. He wants to know that a person also cares about food, and that he or she understands that the wine is meant to go with the food, not the other way around. And, like Amanda, he never forgets that wine is an agricultural production: "Wine *is* food," he says.

He also understands the importance of what might be called the psychology of the sommelier—the necessity of reading his guests and their moods, of meeting them where they are, of listening to them. "Read the customer. Be there when they want you to be there. Listen to the customer, and hear what he has to say." Reading a customer also means knowing when not to hover, when to be almost invisible (while keeping an eye).

"How pliable are they?" Roger wants to know of would-be sommeliers. "Can they be taught to talk to people about wine without coming across as arrogant or snooty? This can be difficult—a little knowledge can be dangerous!"

If faced with a difficult customer, can this person disarm them? Can he or she make adjustments to put them at ease, and let them know they're in good hands? Above all, what Roger wants from sommeliers is elegantly simple: "You have to be helpful."

Roger took to teaching quickly, and it has remained a vital part of his professional life; he recently celebrated twenty years as an instructor at the New York City College of Technology. But he also thrives on the restaurant floor. It energizes him, and it has been part of his existence since he was a teenager. It's like home. After one year working full-time at FCI, he returned to Tse Yang, where his second stint lasted about three years.

In the early 1990s, Roger got a phone call from Karen Waltuck, who owned the restaurant Chanterelle with her husband, the chef David Waltuck. Chanterelle wasn't new: it had opened in Soho in 1979, and moved to a grander space in Tribeca in 1989. Thomas Keller, best known now as the chef and owner of California's French Laundry, had suggested that Karen call Roger, whom he had met at a wine event, when she was seeking recommendations for a new sommelier. Roger himself initially wasn't interested: He'd been toying with the idea of moving down south with his wife and kids, and opening a place of his own. But he knew and admired Chanterelle enough not to rule it out altogether.

Roger made a recommendation to Karen, but that sommelier left the restaurant after two years to become a wine rep. Karen called Roger again, for another referral. He had not packed in and headed south, and this time around he said, "I'm interested."

He stayed at Chanterelle until it closed in 2009, almost sixteen years after he took the job.

If any restaurant could be said to match Le Pont Neuf for specialness—for the love and compassion and kindness of which that Le Pont Neuf regular spoke—it would be Chanterelle. Karen and David Waltuck are "the most wonderful people," Roger tells me without hesitating even for a moment to choose his words, and the restaurant they ran together was "magical." They sought out and cultivated staff who were unusual, even a little quirky, but unstintingly professional, and who came to feel that they worked with the Waltucks, not for them. On my visits to the restaurant with Frank, we noted that palpable sense of camaraderie and cooperation among the staff. No wonder, then, that even Chanterelle's "family meals" were legendary, good enough to warrant a cookbook of their own, *Staff Meals at Chanterelle*.

Roger would become a beloved and integral member of the Chanterelle family, and the Waltucks extended to him the trust and freedom to create the kind of list he thought would work best at their restaurant, a list that would offer its customers not only familiar bottles they already knew they loved, but new ones to discover—along with sake and rum and other liquid pleasures that Roger's expertise and authority encompassed. The Waltucks' faith in Roger had not been misplaced: three months after he started at the restaurant, it was elevated from a two- to a four-star review in the *New York Times* (the one in which Ruth Reichl commended Roger's unintimidating, even affectionate, style). It was in 1996, during his time at Chanterelle, that Roger won the James Beard Foundation award for Outstanding Wine Service, the highest honor it bestows in the field.

And just as his father had at Le Pont Neuf, Roger organized memorable dinners that revolved around wines he loved and the interesting people who produced them. Every restaurant where he worked, including his first, helped to shape his style and sensibility. But my sense is that, in Chanterelle, he found the right fit both for his talent and his gentle personality.

After Chanterelle closed in 2009, wounding the hearts of many of its regulars and the people who worked there, just as so many had been crushed when Le Pont Neuf closed, Roger didn't lack for job opportunities. He spent three years at Porter House, an upscale steakhouse near Lincoln Center. Then he went to Tocqueville, a refined, somewhat discreet modern French restaurant, and its Japanese sister, 15 East (which had nearly one hundred sakes on its list), and served as beverage director for both restaurants. He even reunited with David Waltuck at his short-lived restaurant, Élan, where he created its first wine list, served as a consultant, and occasionally worked on the floor during wine events. By the time Élan closed in 2016, Roger had spent more than forty years working in restaurants, mostly as a sommelier, not including his adolescent employment in his family's restaurant. He had a distinguished teaching career, too. Maybe this would be a natural time to extricate himself from the rigors of the dining room floor. Maybe not.

## 6

At Roberta's, Amanda Smeltz was part of an unusual restaurant environment, one that showed people that they could "walk into this concrete, dilapidated, ugly building on a deserted corner, and all of your servers are not only tattooed, but wearing God-knows-what they found in their weird closet that day, and you're going to be served some of the most delicious pizza in New York," she says. "You're going to have a bizarrely delicious meal while sitting on a bench, with punishing death metal on. It's a disorienting experience—and you're accidentally going to be drinking one of the loveliest bottles of wine you could possibly get for fifty-five bucks."

For a time, it was a great fit. But four years in, things

were changing. The people in charge wanted to expand, and open another restaurant. There were internal conflicts. "It wasn't just that I was ready to move on," she says, but that she was concerned about the direction in which the restaurant was heading. "I didn't necessarily want to hitch my wagon to this forever." Parting ways wasn't easy. "It bummed me out a lot," she remembers, adding, as though she were discussing the end of a long romance, "I thought they were the one."

But there was another issue. For Amanda, to whom constant learning is so essential, there was no one at Roberta's for her to learn from—and she would never dare to think she has nothing left to learn. "Well, what's next?" she thought. "What do I do?" She found out that the sommelier Michael Madrigale was leaving his post at Bar Boulud and Boulud Sud. An email had gone out from Daniel Johnnes (himself an esteemed sommelier), the corporate wine director of Dinex, the French chef Daniel Boulud's restaurant group, saying they needed to make a hire. "And I thought, 'what the hell?' Just throw this at the wall and see what sticks."

If I were asked to think of a New York City restaurant that might be the opposite of Roberta's, I might present one of Daniel Boulud's places as a contender. They're in

Manhattan, for starters—most of them many zip codes and tax brackets away from Bushwick. You will not find a rickety bench, an outdoor tiki bar, or a waiter in a tattered death-metal t-shirt in any of them. Still, what Roberta's and the Boulud joints do have in common are high-quality food, service, and wine—even if stylistically they could hardly be more different.

She talked to the people at Dinex, and they asked her to give it a shot. "So I went back into fine dining. And I spent a year figuring out and deciding if I could inhabit that kind of wine environment again. And wondering if I could bring the types of wine that I care for very much to that space, and how they would do."

I'm surprised to learn that that wasn't a primary, or even secondary, reason why Amanda got the Boulud gig; I assumed they wanted someone who would shake things up. I assumed they understood her sensibility from the start. "I'm not so sure," Amanda says. "I think the reason that they liked me was that I was an operator. I was single-handedly operating two notable businesses and making a lot of money for that company." Her devotion to natural winemaking might not have been a decisive factor in the hiring, or a factor at all, but it was clear that she could manage a $350,000 cellar. "I was largely left alone for that year as long as I was operating smoothly. So I bought a bunch of natural wine and put it in the cellar along with all of these big, blue-chip wines. The cool thing about that is that some of the blue-chip wines are also naturally produced. So there's this interesting spectrum where some farmers never changed their ways, and their wines are from famous places like the Rhone Valley and Burgundy, but they always farmed well. So there were some of those wines in the cellar: My grandfather did it this way, my father did it this way, and if it ain't broke, we're not changing it."

Along with the reminder that staggeringly costly, blue-chip bottles could be very, very good, Amanda was also reminded that customers can be surprising, and that some of the older, more affluent diners who made up much of Boulud's clientele could be just as open as her customers at Roberta's. Still, she decided that the job wasn't the best fit for her.

Amanda had started thinking seriously about opening a place of her own during her last year at Roberta's. After leaving the Boulud restaurants and contemplating the possibility of launching a wine bar on the Lower East Side, she took six months off from the restaurant business and wrote a business plan. "It was the first time I ever did that. It was also the first time I hadn't been in a restaurant job in eight years, or something like that." But it wasn't yet the right time. "The amount of money we needed to raise to get that wine bar off the ground just ended up being too much. We tried for six months, and it was a very good practice for me, and an extremely useful exercise. Because no one teaches you that stuff. You have to go learn it for yourself." For now, the wine bar would have to wait.

SOMMELIER LIFE, I LEARNED from both Amanda and Roger, can be a distinctly transient life: long engagements like Roger's at Chanterelle seem to be more the exception than the rule. Part of this might result from the risks and complexities of restaurants themselves; many simply don't last long. But part of it might also come from the nature of the work, and the nature of the people who do it. They're curious. They like to be challenged. They want to try new and different things. They want to grow. And sometimes, like the rest of us, they just have to trust and follow their instincts.

Amanda heard that Louis Fabbrini was leaving Café Altro Paradiso and Estela, and moving to Los Angeles. She counts Louis as a friend, and admires him as a colleague. They're similar in style and sensibility. She knew she'd be walking into "a pretty cool cellar."

Estela and Café Altro Paradiso occupy an appealing middle ground between Roberta's and the Boulud restaurants. They are in Manhattan, but they are downtown. They allow for, and even encourage, some experimentation with both food and wine. They are certainly more formal than Roberta's—but less straitlaced than Bar Boulud. They are neither for the young, nor the old, but some of each (and, as I observed the night I trailed Amanda, many diners—perhaps a majority—fall somewhere in the middle).

In contrast to her experiences at Roberta's and the Boulud restaurants, Amanda didn't make any radical changes when she landed at Altro Paradiso and Estela. "It's such a pleasure to walk into someone's house where you feel like they're kindred spirits," she says. There was no need for a major overhaul, or for establishing a point of view; it was already in place. "Here, it's just fine-tuning. Maybe I'll have a little more emphasis on this section of the wine list. I like this region a little bit more than Louis. Things like that. It's very much a dialogue between his work and my work, which is lovely."

Estela is a magnet for those who want to drink natural wines—but that doesn't mean that everyone who dines there is automatically on board with the ideological program (remember the European couple, who knew quite a lot about wine, but whose canonical taste differed in a fundamental way from the character of the restaurant's list), or that they are even aware that it exists. It is entirely possible to have a great night at Estela without knowing or caring about viticulture, small production, soil maintenance, or fermentation methods. But Amanda would like you to take an interest, and she notices that more and more customers are doing just that. They're very inquisitive about natural winemaking, and Amanda wants to engage them and have that conversation. "It's connected to the whole movement of reexamining our agriculture globally," she says. If people are already accustomed to knowing the difference between organically farmed produce and conventionally farmed produce when they're doing their grocery shopping, it's not a huge leap for them to see how that applies to wine, too. "They're finally starting to connect the finished wine to fruit. It's a really big deal. There's a new dialogue happening," Amanda says. Not so long ago, a customer might have seemed eccentric if she asked for a natural wine. That's changing.

"I had a woman look up at me last night and say with hesitation, like, you don't happen to have any, any biodynamic or any naturally farmed wines on this wine list do you? And I was like, yes, all of them."

AMANDA IS PUTTING HER stamp on Estela's list in other ways, too. When she tastes a wine that moves her, she wants to bring it to her customers—and, in the process, diversify the list even further. There hadn't been any American wines on the list, and she's getting ready to introduce some. One is a merlot (if *that movie* made you dismiss this venerable and excellent grape, it's time to get over it, please) from Sonoma—and I can tell Amanda is pretty excited that someone there is making wine the way she prefers it to be made. "They're in a minority, but it's happening more and more, and you want it to happen more and more." And many of Estela's international guests have signed on to the buy local, eat local, drink local program—which means they'd love to try some American wine when they're out to dinner in New York City.

The other American wine she's putting on the list is a Gewürztraminer from the Columbia River Gorge in the Pacific Northwest—a region she visited that made a powerful impression on her.

She normally takes two research trips per year, which enrich her work more than I had conjectured: "Visiting a vineyard changes everything," she tells me. There's no substitute for spending a few hours walking the vineyards with a winemaker, having lunch at their table, listening to them discuss their relation to their region. It's a crucial part of an education in wine—not just a benefit, but a necessity.

When one has spent time with a farmer, a winemaker, a family, a bottle of wine becomes something more than a bottle of wine. "It's the representation of people's work. A missive from their home."

I'M THINKING BACK NOW to the wine class I sat in on at Estela, the day after I trailed Amanda, and months before she told me firsthand about how much her visits to vineyards matter to her work. That day, I got a close look at her frankly brilliant style as an educator—and at how her teaching excellence not only informs her colleagues, but also energizes them.

She leads a wine class at both of her restaurants, Estela and Altro Paradiso, every week. Unlike many other classes she teaches, for which she's established a clear, organizing principle—by geography, say, or style, or grape—this one was a bit of an outlier, whose theme essentially was, "white wines that are hard to sell." Like the Falkenstein she rhapsodized about the previous night right before service, these are bottles she loves and believes in, and she'd like her customers to love them, too.

Amanda begins by outlining the three reasons these wines pose a challenge. The first is simply that they are white: for a variety of reasons that probably aren't fair at all, it is a widely held belief that white wines are lower in quality, somehow less important, than red wines. The second is trickier and less concrete: these wines have "challenging profiles." People tend to pay more for a name they know—whether it's the name of the winery, the grape, the type of wine. The third is that they're more expensive than many other white wines on the list—all are at least $90—and while diners at Estela might not blink at a $100 price tag on a bottle of red, they're not quite willing to shell out that much on a bottle of white; Amanda points out that people are generally willing to spend $20 to $30 more per bottle on red.

The wines under scrutiny this afternoon are, she says, "white wines nobody knows!" hailing from four regions in three countries, the Czech Republic, Germany, and Italy. White wines from France are easier to sell (remember the Blazers' request for a white Burgundy). Italy might be a little less of a stretch for some guests than the other two countries represented today. "Our ideas of wine lists change historically," Amanda explains. She has studied the menus of some of New York's venerated restaurants of yesteryear (there's an excellent archive of these at the New York Public Library). Before World War II, such menus were loaded with German Rieslings; during the war, a bias against German wines took hold, and it has persisted. And if you mention Czech wine to just about anyone, you'll be met with either a blank or incredulous look.

In some ways these little-known white wines are studies in subtlety versus power, Amanda suggests. "Subtlety is a different value in wine," she says. It's a quality I often look for, and respond to, in wines—but a difficult one to articulate. Subtlety is expressed, Amanda continues, in "layering, gradation, gentleness." As at most wine tastings, we will move from lightest to heaviest today.

To disclose in detail here everything that transpired in less than two hours of wine class with Amanda isn't possible, as it could easily fill a book of its own—I'm imagining a beautiful little monograph on a single master class with a master teacher. But I learned a lot in that short time, and I'd like to share at least some of what I took away:

I learned that terraced old vineyards are special, and almost "impossible to farm." Each individual step in the terrace is simply too narrow to accommodate the machinery that makes industrial winemaking easier—and sometimes the whole of the terrace is itself just too steep. These are grapes that must be tended, and taken, by hand.

I learned about the grape variety Sylvaner, which is grown mainly in Germany and France's Alsace region and whose name, just like the English *sylvan*, speaks of woodlands and pastoral idylls and thereby delights me. "If chardonnay and Riesling had a baby," Amanda summarizes, "it would be sylvaner." The sample we taste is from wine-maker Stefan Vetter, in Germany's Franken region. Vetter is committed to biodynamics—that most mystical school of agricultural theory and practice, rooted in ideas developed by the Austrian philosopher Rudolf Steiner, which is atten-tive to the phases of the moon and sympathetic magic. The wine is fermented in wood, and is bottled unfiltered. "It has dimension," Amanda says, and for something so subtle, real backbone, even a meaty quality. Going around the table, her colleagues detect something smoky, maybe some caraway, a hint of fennel. A German server is clearly psyched about this wine, which she thinks would be terrific with that German comfort-food classic, sauerbraten. Amanda agrees—and points out that it is also excellent with the single food that most notoriously eludes and evades pairing: asparagus. So now you know: there is a wine that goes with asparagus.

I learned about the winemaker Eva Fricke, who makes a Riesling called Krone—"old woman"—in the Rheingau, a wine that is "silky and forceful," and about as high in acidity as a wine can go. It would not be out of order to recommend it to someone who asks for a white burgundy. It would be excellent with raw seafood. Even raw beef. If Vetter's wines might be called "folksy," Fricke's are "aristocratic" and "very elegant." (It is around this time that one of the servers invokes Marx and Hegel, and Amanda does not object to their presence in the conversation.)

I learned about a young Czech winemaker named Milan Nestarec, who took over his father's winery and is about as hands-off as one can be. His grapes are organic. He weeds only twice a year. He lets lots of stuff grow amid the vines: grass, and wildflowers. He makes a chardonnay that does not look like a chardonnay. It could be great with endive. Salty cheese. Fish sauce. It might be a chardonnay that goes with steak.

I learned about Franco Terpin's vineyard, near Trieste, composed of about nine hectares, all cared for and harvested by hand. It produces a Sauvignon Blanc of notable body and texture. There's some brine. Some leather. Some resin. And memorably, to one server's palate, it's a bit like what might happen if you were to "dip a sardine in jam."

Amanda receives this great variety of gustatory analysis with satisfaction. No one is wrong. Some language is more colorful, perhaps more subjective, than other. Some similes might seem to stretch. But there can be no doubt that everyone at the table is really thinking about the wines, focusing on them, and using the best and most truthful words they can muster to talk about them. And they are talking about them with joy and good humor. Selling these wines might not be easy, but around this table, it seems like it will, at least, be fun to try.

It isn't until our conversation months later that I find out that Amanda has visited all of the makers of all of the wines tasted and smelled and scrutinized during that class (with the exception of Franco Terpin), and that I understand how profoundly in-person encounters affected her. It would not be possible for every sommelier and server at Estela to travel to Germany, Hungary, and Moravia—but, as I had been told by Emily the maître d' the night before this class, teaching is Amanda's "other calling," and she's so deft at it at that it's as though she can transmit her affection, her knowledge, and the lived experience of learning directly from those winemakers on their home turf to the rest of the floor staff. But she doesn't want the sommeliers and servers to mimic what she says. She encourages them to be themselves, to use their own language, to own their opinions.

A sommelier is, at heart, a communicator. She knows things that most of us don't know, and a great portion of her job is to share that knowledge with us in a comprehensible, engaging, and useful way. There are some people for whom clear, compelling communication seems to come easily. "It's easier for them to connect what they're experiencing with articulated thought, which is the hardest part of the somm job," Amanda says. "You have to help customers find language to communicate what they're looking for, what they enjoy. You have to be the one to guide them to that language. And then you also have to be the interpreter of other people's language about sensate experience."

There is, she continues, "a certain amount of mental horsepower and intuitiveness that I think the work actually requires. You have to be attentive to your own senses, and you also have to be able to connect language to those experiences."

Brittany and Keara, the two younger, junior sommeliers at Estela whom Amanda has mentored throughout their careers, "have very different ways of talking about wine and the way that they experience it. Brittany will often keep her analytic responses to herself. She instead will be much more impressionistic, more encouraging when she helps people think about and talk about wines, way more playful." Keara, on the other hand, is very precise, polished, and exacting with her language—but she's "so warm and communicative" that customers trust her.

I've been to many wine tastings, and to a few wine classes,

here and there. Amanda's is the liveliest and most interesting I've ever attended, by far. I want to invite myself back, every week. But I sense that that would be an intrusion. It pleased me to consider that Amanda's wine class reminded me of my favorite poetry classes in college. Without undermining its beauty or soul, she brought clarity to a complex subject, working through each bottle as though it was a text she was submitting to a close reading. And, as with poetry, understanding a wine is fine, but feeling it matters more.

I ADMIT TO AMANDA that there is a reactionary part of me that says if the wine is delicious and the food is delicious, everything will work out fine. If I like a certain light-bodied pinot noir, and I like steak, I am not going to worry about the burly rib-eye overpowering the delicate flower of a wine. Is it possible that we make too much of a fuss over pairing food and wine?

This, I know, is an absurd thing to say to a sommelier, whose work demands that they pair food and wine in the interest of giving a customer a pleasurable, perhaps even memorable, experience. But Amanda humors me. "The rule is always drink what you want." However she maintains that there are "structural dimensions to wine and to food" that also play a part in successful pairing. She's thinking of factors like these: how acidity works, or how the presence of oak might affect the flavor of a dish. Inherently, I know that we are both right, but I concede that she is more right than I am. Yes, of course it is fine to drink what you want to drink with whatever it is you want to eat. But I do know from experience the delicious play between just the right wine and just the right cheese, or the lift a heavy dish gets from a crisp, bright white, or, for that matter, the unthinkable prospect of enjoying a hot dog without a beer.

I remember Roger talking about how much he has learned from making mistakes. Estela seems like a great place to be working with wine—but also exceptionally challenging; it's like "Pairing 301," Amanda says. Has she ever made any serious missteps? "Oh sure. Many times," she tells me. "Multiple times." What does failure look like for a sommelier? It can take a few different forms, but at its core it means not giving customers a great experience with food and wine.

That black rice has been on my mind since the night I trailed Amanda. That freaking rice that everybody eats at Estela. I tell Amanda that I wouldn't even know where to begin as far as pairing it with wine goes. And I realize that this is where my seemingly democratic, simplified theory of wine and food falters. I know that just because I happen to like the rice, and I happen to like a particular pinot noir, none of this means that they're going to hit it off. In fact, I have a powerful hunch that they won't.

"It is so huge, it is so intense, and it usually happens two-thirds of the way through the meal, which drives me bananas, bananas!" she says, because it utterly defies what we think of as a standard progression of wine during a meal, from light to heavy. "Just forget it, because the black rice is a crusher. It's a total crusher. It knocks out all of my white wines by the glass except for one: a really oxidative chenin blanc from really old vines in the center of the Loire Valley somehow stands up to it." Up against this black and crusty fish-sauce flavor bomb, this wine is perfect: it has enough muscle.

This is what she means about food and wine pairing. She knows that that wine works with the black rice because she understands how oxidization works in white wine, and knows how it interacts with food. She has also, of course, put her theory into practice: She has eaten the rice, together with the wine, and has pronounced it not only good—but very good.

IF THE TIME COMES when Amanda decides to leave Estela and Café Altro Paradiso, I'm sure she won't lack for job offers. Or maybe that's when she'll be able to open that wine bar of her own at last. Where does she envision herself five years from now? What will she be doing? Right now, she sees three distinct possibilities.

One is that, yes, she'll revisit the wine bar dream for which she'd drawn up that business plan a few years ago—but this time she'll find the capital.

Another is that she will continue to grow at her current restaurant group, developing even greater autonomy and leadership in the business.

And the third is the most radical: That she'll find some old vines, and tend to them herself—maybe in Catalonia: She's captivated by the region's history and its wines. She admires the "openhearted, tough" farmers she's met there. She loves its "spectrum of people," and what she perceives as its communitarian spirit. But she is also rightly sensitive to what it might mean to be an outsider there, to what kind of impact she might make. "Where can I do the most good?"

I see virtues in all of these possibilities, but as a hopeless Romantic, of course I like the Catalonia idea best of all. Wherever she lands, whatever she decides to do, I know that writing poetry will still be part of the plan, too. It has to be.

After all, I'd been drawn to Amanda because I knew her reputation as a smart sommelier with a clear point of view and a down-to-earth approach to her work—and because I also knew that she was a serious poet.

For all of its rigors, being a sommelier is a more dependable way to make a living than being a poet—and Amanda has carved out a good life in the profession, while still writing poetry (even if she wishes she could devote much more time to the craft).

"What's harder for your family? Poetry or wine?" I ask.

"Oh God. Honestly, poetry."

"You really baffled them on both counts."

"I don't know how it happened, honestly. I don't know. Poetry is still harder."

"But they have your book, surely?"

"One of my brothers does," she says. As for her parents, "It's just not in their wheelhouse. They weren't raised with it, you know. My mom reads," but not poetry.

"I'm sure they're proud of you," I say, and I mean it.

Amanda is quiet for a minute, thinking.

"They're proud that I am able to survive in New York and make money. That's no small feat, you know. They're like, 'Well, we didn't know how you were going to do it, but you seem to be doing it. We're proud of you.' And you know what? I'll take it. That's not a small thing."

# AFTERWORD

What does it take to become a good, and success-ful, sommelier? After spending time with Amanda Smeltz and Roger Dagorn, what I've learned is that the main thing is this: hard work. Being a sommelier is physically taxing. It is organizationally challenging (being good at systems helps). It is also intellectually demanding, but this is one of its foremost pleasures. Roger prepared diligently for exams that granted him certain professional qualifications; Amanda did not. But both have put in countless hours of study in pursuit of excellence in their chosen field. "There is a lot of reading," Amanda says, "and I do think that those people who will become very good at wine are people who don't mind scholarship." (And remember that Roger often stayed awake until four in the morning studying when he decided to become a sommelier.)

Study hard, work hard—and seek out mentors. Amanda had the good fortune of working with Peter Donahue at a formative time in her career; Roger had the advantage of a de facto apprenticeship in his family's restaurant. But both also have benefited from less straightforward mentor relationships, such as Roger's with his colleague and study partner, Larry Stone. Amanda also points to people in the world of wine with whom she did not work directly, but whose generosity and patience and style and knowledge all influenced her approach to her job; among them are Paul Grieco of New York's Terroir wine bars and Hearth restaurant, and Juliette Pope, whose time at Gramercy Tavern has become almost synonymous with its relaxed, unintimidating, professional style.

Drink responsibly. Roger took pains to make a point that should have been obvious to me, but which I confess I hadn't even considered. From my own years in the field, I knew that excessive drinking is an occupational hazard among bartenders. Roger says that same is true among sommeliers. He advises that those who go into the profession exercise caution, and restraint—which isn't always easy in an environment, and a culture, where great quantities of alcohol are always at hand. Drinking wine may seem more sophisticated, more grown up, and less perilous than downing shots of cheap whiskey—but it can still get you drunk.

Mitigate intimidation, and minimize embarrassment. Fear of sommeliers persists, but a good sommelier can do a lot to alleviate it. Amanda's rubric—would my family feel welcomed here?—is an instructive one. And the way Roger Dagorn treated me at Chanterelle when I was an adjunct instructor at the community college around the corner from the restaurant—that is to say, just like everyone else in the restaurant—made an impression that has not faded in a quarter of a century.

Listen to people. Take care of them.

Take care of yourself, too.

Give people space when they want it.

Tell good stories. Be kind.

As I write this, Amanda Smeltz can still be found working like mad at Café Altro Paradiso and Estela, and writing poetry.

As for Roger Dagorn, a few years ago he gave some thought to retiring from the restaurant business. But the gravitational pull of the dining room floor was too powerful for him to resist for long: as much as he enjoyed his work as a teacher, and as happy as he was to have more time to spend with his wife and children and grandchildren, he felt that "something was missing."

So when his old friend Joe Delissio, the wine director at

Brooklyn's famously romantic River Café, gave him a call to see if he might be persuaded to return to the floor as a sommelier, it really didn't take much persuading.

His responsibilities are less rigorous than they were when he was a wine director, and that suits him fine. He works two or three nights a week, much less than he once did. It doesn't feel like a step down—it feels good, and it still gives him more time to spend with his family. The physicality of working on the floor isn't easy for sommeliers in their forties—even as an experienced bartender, one night trailing Amanda at Estela and my feet and my back felt it, hard. Roger is seventy, and the River Café, which is a barge in the East River, poses unique challenges when its springy wood floor rises and falls with the tides. But Roger still loves the work.

The floor, Roger tells me, is "where my heart is"—as if it didn't show.

# FURTHER READING

There are many books that might be useful to aspiring sommeliers. But given the vastness of the subject of wine, Amanda Smeltz recommends an interesting approach to beginning a course of study: pick a region that appeals to you, and learn as much about is you can. That way, you'll get a sense of place, of the science of that place, of the historical forces that shaped it, and, in turn, shaped its viticulture. (One excellent recent example that I can think of is *Champagne: The Essential Guide to the Wines, Producers, and Terroirs of the Iconic Region*, by Peter Liem.)

The list that follows is much more generalist in nature. This short list skims the surface—a selection of books about wine that I have found instructive, delightful, or, in the best cases, both. None of these were written to serve as training manuals for aspiring sommeliers, but all can deepen one's knowledge of wine—even in cases when one finds oneself arguing against an author.

Eric Asimov, *How to Love Wine*. Asimov is direct,
  unpretentious, and evenhanded—and, like a good
  sommelier, he wants you to feel comfortable drinking
  wine and talking about it, and he wants you to love it.
Hugh Johnson and Jancis Robinson, *The World Atlas of Wine*. It
  is essential to have at least one good atlas, and this is my
  favorite of its kind.
Kermit Lynch, *Adventures on the Wine Route: A Wine Buyer's
  Tour of France*. A respected importer's reflections on his
  life in the business and the wines he loves.
Jay McInerney, *A Hedonist in the Cellar* and *The Juice: Vinous
  Veritas*. The former is a collection of the well-known
  novelist's wine columns for *House & Garden* magazine. The
  latter includes essays for that and other periodicals.
Jancis Robinson, *The Oxford Companion to Wine*. Another very
  useful reference book.

There are also great websites out there for students of wine. I've
found these two especially useful:

  SevenFiftyDaily, to which Amanda Smeltz has
    contributed articles.
  The Feiring Line. Alice Feiring is arguably natural wine's
    most voluble champion, so her website is an excellent
    place to dive deeply into that category.

# ACKNOWLEDGMENTS

When I first heard from Stuart Roberts, this book's editor, I told him that I'd always wanted to write a book for Simon & Schuster—because I would not exist were it not for the company.

That's not hyperbole. My late and very beloved maternal grandparents, Lester and Henrietta Gottlieb, met when they worked for Simon & Schuster in its early years: he was the "office boy" (presumably now an obsolete role) and she was an administrator so formidable that, she claimed, it took five people to replace her when she left. So, thank you, Grandpa and Grandma: how I wish you were here to see this.

And thank you, Stuart, not only for that thrilling initial email but for being so genial, diligent, perceptive, and patient from start to finish. It has been a pleasure.

I'm grateful to Sean Manning at Simon & Schuster and Ashley Lopez at Waxman Literary Agency. To the staff of Estela. And to Eric Asimov, Jami Attenberg, Sandra Bark, Rosita Boland, Katie

Freeman, Laurie Gunst, Imogene Jaffe, Bob and Sylvia Jorlette, Shawn Kelley, Winter Miller, Jeremy Schaap, Tucker Schwarz, Michael Sharkey, Joe and Nancy Silvio, René Steinke, Annika Sundvik, Jeffrey Walkowiak, and Susan Zugaib.

Of course the greatest portion of my gratitude belongs to Roger Dagorn and Amanda Smeltz, whom I thank with a full heart for sharing their time, experience, and insight with me. I couldn't possibly admire you more, as professionals and as people. You really are the finest teachers, and I loved every minute I spent in your company.

## ABOUT THE AUTHOR

Rosie Schaap is the author of *Drinking with Men: A Memoir*. From 2011 to 2017, she was the "Drink" columnist for *The New York Times Magazine*, and she has also written for publications including *Lucky Peach*, *Saveur*, *The New York Times Book Review*, and *Travel + Leisure*. Schaap is a contributor to *This American Life*, and her essays have been widely anthologized. She was previously and variously employed as a community organizer, an editor, a manager of homeless shelters, and, for many years, a bartender.